SHIVA

Dictations received by the Messenger
Tatyana Nicholaevna Mickushina
from 2005 through 2016

UDC 141.339=111=03.161.1
BBC 87.7+86.4

M59 Mickushina, T.N.
SHIVA.
Masters of Wisdom. – T.N. Mickushina. –
– 2017. – 161 c. – ("Masters of Wisdom" series).

This book continues the Masters of Wisdom series of books.

This series of books presents a collection of Messages from different Masters who are most well-known to modern humanity. These Messages were transmitted through the Messenger Tatyana N. Mickushina, who has been working under the guidance of the Masters of Wisdom since 2004. Using a special method, T. N. Mickushina has received Messages from over 50 Beings of Light.

The present volume contains selected Messages of Lord Shiva. Many Teachings are given in these Messages; including the Teaching about God, the Teaching about Discernment of reality from illusion: which helps to ascend to a new level of consciousness and also new aspects of the Guru-chela relationship are considered.

UDC 141.339
BBC 87.7+86.4

ISBN-10: 1546678379
ISBN-13:978-1546678373

Contents

4

Shiva - the good Lord

Shiva is one of the most well-known gods of India. Together with Brahma and Vishnu, He is part of the Hindu Trinity – Trimurti. Shiva, Brahma, and Vishnu are considered three manifestations of the One Higher Being. They are "three in one," corresponding to the undivided essence of the western Trinity: the Father, the Son, and the Holy Spirit Brahma personifies the Creator aspect of God; Vishnu - the Preserver and the defender; and Shiva - the Destroyer and the annihilator.

Shiva embodies all of these aspects for Hindus who choose him as their Supreme God. Shiva's followers worship him as the Supreme Reality, the absolute Godhead. They see in him the Guru of all gurus, the destroyer of worldliness, ignorance, evil, villainy, hatred and diseases. He bestows wisdom and longevity, embodies self-renunciation and compassion.

The name "Shiva" originates from the Sanskrit word meaning "good," "kind," and "friendly." The diversity of Shiva's aspects is reflected in His many names. Thus, the Hindu sacred text called "Shiva Purana," cites 1008 different names of Shiva. One of them is Shambhu, which means "gracious" or "bringing happiness." Another name, Shankara, means "giving joy" or "beneficial." As

Mahadev, He is a "great god." Ishvara (Master), a name of Shiva that means He possesses all glory inherent in the Divine

Pashupati is another of His names which means "Master of the cattle." As Master of the cattle, Shiva is a shepherd or pastor of souls. Shiva is depicted riding a white bull, whose name is Nandi, meaning "joyful." According to Hindu tradition, Nandi was a human, one of the followers of Shiva who took the form of a bull because his human body wasn't strong enough to contain his religious ecstasy occurring in the presence of Shiva.

The bull Nandi is depicted in the majority of Shiva temples. Usually he sits looking at Lord Shiva. Nandi symbolizes the human soul, aspiring to God. He also represents the soul, immersed in deep contemplation of Shiva as the Absolute Reality. Shiva helps us to reveal our Absolute Reality.

The mountain Kailash is Shiva's throne and also the location of His paradisiacal country. This majestic mountain is the highest peak of the Kailash Range in the Tibetan Himalayas. Hindus worship Kailash as the most sacred mountain in the world and they make pilgrimages there.

Shiva is full of contrasts. He symbolizes both contemplation and action. He is often portrayed as a beggar yogi immersed in deep meditation.

Legends say that Shiva walks around the earth with a bowl for handouts. He teaches that renunciation, rejection of attachments, indifference to success and failure - all of these are ways to Him.

Shiva is known also as Mrityunjaya - One who conquers death. He is also Kamare, the Destroyer of desires. These two names demonstrate that he, who destroys desires, can defeat death, because desires give birth to actions, actions give birth to consequences, consequences give birth to dependence and lack of freedom, which result in new birth leading to death.

As Maha Yogi, or great yogi, Shiva is the King of all yogis, the highest embodiment of the spirit of asceticism.

Shiva also personifies the moving Universe. In the Hindu sacred text "Kurma Purana", Shiva says: "I am a creator, God, residing in the state of Highest Bliss; I am the Yogi, eternally dancing the Cosmic Dance."

According to Hindu beliefs, Shiva executes an array of various dances. One of them is called Tandava, the dance of creation and destruction. While dancing, Shiva leads the Universe into manifestation, supports it, and then, at the end of an era, while dancing, takes it away from its emergence. Shiva is the embodiment of Ananda (Supreme Bliss). The divine dance, Tandava, originates out of this cosmic ecstasy which Lord Shiva performs using all of Space as a stage.

The most famous image of Shiva is the image of Nataraja, the King of Dancers, or the Lord of Dance. Nataraja dances in the golden palace at the center of the Universe. This golden palace represents the human heart. One of the Hindu hymns glorifying Shiva's dance says: "dancing, he appears in an immaculate lotus of the heart."

The relationship between Shiva and His followers bears a very personal character. Despite the fact that he lives on Mount Kailash, His favorite dwelling place is in the hearts of the devoted.

According to Hindu tradition, when the gods decided to let the river Ganges descend from Heaven, in order to prevent the destruction of the Earth, Lord Shiva calmly absorbed the blow of the falling water onto His head. Having trapped the river in His hair, he let Ganga out in small streams, splitting it into seven sacred rivers.

For Hindus, the Ganges represents a refreshing river of spiritual wisdom. According to Hindu tradition, when the gods decided to let the river Ganges descend from Heaven, Shiva was in the center of the whirlpool of light - the energy rotating around him – was the balancing factor between heaven and earth as the onrushing river of light crystallized and became terrestrial. Therefore, Hindus consider the waters of the river Ganges sacred, magical and purifying for everything. The Ascended Masters teach that these seven sacred rivers also represent seven beams of Holy Spirit, coming from the white light.

The role of Shiva corresponds to the role of the Holy Spirit in the western Trinity.

In the ancient text it is said: "Comprehend the meaning of an image which Shiva has taken for people to worship Him. In His throat, Shiva holds the deadly poison, Halhala, capable of destroying all life. On His head is the sacred river, Ganges, whose life giving waters can purify and heal all diseases everywhere (for Ganga represents the nectar of immortality). On His forehead a fiery eye (the eye of wisdom). On His head is the cool and soothing Moon (the crescent indicating His complete control of the mind). On His wrists, ankles, shoulders, and neck He wears deadly cobras that feed on the life-giving air (prana)." Ordinary people are frightened by the sight of snakes, but Shiva adorns His body with them. This means that Lord Shiva is completely free from fear and is immortal. Snakes, as a rule, live hundreds of years. The snakes swirling on Shiva's body symbolize to us that He is Eternal.

Shiva is an example of great patience and endurance. He holds poison in His throat, that according to legend, He drank so as to save all life on earth from being poisoned. On His head He carries the blessed Moon, which everyone greets with joy. An important lesson can be learned from this: one should not project/ spew out his bad qualities and tendencies on others, rather, everything useful and kind in one's possession should be used for the good and wellbeing of all.

There are three strips of bhasma or vibhuti on Shiva's forehead.[1] The meaning of this silent reminder

___

[1] Bhasma and vibhuti – the sacred ashes used in Hindu rituals (Wikipedia).

is that it is necessary for a human to destroy the three impurities: anava (egoism), karma (action expecting a result), and maya (illusion), and also the three vasana (subtle impressions):

– worldly ("Loka Vasana") - desire of friends, family, power, wealth, glory, honor, respect.

– holy scriptures ("Sastra Vasana") - spiritual arrogance, thoughtless accumulation of knowledge, philosophizing.

– corporal ("Deha Vasana") - desire to have a perfect physique, health, a beautiful face, desire to prolong life with consumption of medications.

Having destroyed these impurities one can approach Lord Shiva, with a pure heart.

Shiva is also symbolically portrayed in the shape of a lingam - a symbol which, in most cases, constitutes a vertically placed cylinder with a rounded or hemispherical top. The word "lingam" originates from the Sanskrit root "'Li," which means "merging" or "dissolution." It is the form in which all other forms dissolve. Shiva is the God blessing all beings with the most desirable gift – merging with the Absolute.

Shiva is the keeper of everything that is necessary for prosperity. He bestows the gift of wisdom. Shiva abides in each thought, word, and action because He is behind all energy, power, and intellect - they are all Him. God manifested as time, space, and causality is inside us.

The exclamation "Shivoham" (I am Shiva) was proclaimed by those souls that learned the truth in a flash of enlightenment after long years of mind purification and selfless devotion. "Shivoham" means "I am Divine."

Shiva's devotees believe that "the Name of Lord Shiva chanted in any way, correctly or incorrectly, knowingly or unknowingly, carefully or carelessly, is sure to give the desired result. The glory of the Name of Lord Shiva cannot be established through reasoning and intellect. It can certainly be experienced or realized only through devotion, faith and constant repetition of the Name and singing His hymns with Bhava."

In his renowned work "Lord Shiva and His Worship," Sri Swami Sivananda (1887 - 1963), a famous Hindu teacher of the 20th century, speaks about the influence of constant repetition of Shiva's names and the hymns devoted to Him:

"The mind is purified by constant repetition of Siva-Stotra[2] and Names of Lord Shiva. The Stotras are filled with good and pure thoughts. Repetition of the hymns to Shiva strengthens the good Samskaras. "As a man thinks, that he becomes". This is the psychological law. The mind of a man who trains himself in thinking good, holy thoughts, develops a tendency to think of good thoughts. His character is molded and transformed by continued good thought. When the mind thinks of the image of the Lord during singing His hymns, the mental substance actually assumes the form of the image of the Lord. The impression of the object thought of is left in the mind. This is called Samskara. When the act is repeated very often, the Samskaras gain strength by repetition, and a tendency or habit is formed in the mind. He who entertains thoughts of Divinity, becomes transformed actually into the Divinity himself by constant thinking. His Bhava or aspiration is purified and divinized. When one sings

---

[2] Stotra (sanscrit. Praise) – an Old Indian hymn-praise (Wikipedia)

the hymns of Lord Shiva, he is in tune with the Lord. The individual mind melts in the cosmic mind. He who sings the hymns becomes one with Lord Siva.

Just as fire has the natural property of consuming all unlike itself, similarly the Name of Lord Shiva has the power of burning sins, Samskaras and Vasanas and bestowing eternal bliss and everlasting peace on those who repeat the Name of the Lord."

References:

1. Mark L. Prophet and Elizabeth Clare Prophet. The Masters and Their Retreats. - m: Moscow, 2006.

2. Sri Svami Sivananda. Lord Shiva and His Worship. Library of the Vedic literature. Penza: the Golden section, 1999.

I have come to give you a Teaching about God because in this world and in all other worlds there is nothing but God. The state of consciousness that you possess now is the only thing that separates you from God and the Divine Truth.

If you meditate on God and the Divine Truth every day, then you will be able to express this Truth in your world more fully and completely.

The task of your embodiment is to enable the Divine Truth to manifest through you, through your entire being!

Lord Shiva,
December 22, 2012

The future of Russia is bound up with the restoration of the traditions of the true faith

April 2, 2005

I AM Shiva! I have come!

I have come to you through this Messenger. I have come!

Shiva is my name. Shiva! I AM Shiva!

In India, which is a faraway country in respect to the so-called western civilized world, I am respected as the Highest Deity. Millions of people worship me, pray to me, and make sacrifices to me.

I am the Supreme God and I have a severe temper. However, I am the best friend of the people devoted to me, and they can spend time in communication with me, enjoy my presence and our mutual communion.

I am very severe with those people who do not respect God and have forgotten about their Divine nature, who do not worship God within and outside them.

God is everything. God is everything surrounding you as far as you can see. You are God too. Yes, you are God in incarnation, but your Divine nature can

18

be manifested only when you meet certain demands necessary for this.

I will tell you what you have to do in order to become God.

First of all, you should love and respect God in everything surrounding you. There is nothing in the world separating you from other particles of life irrespective of whether it is a tiny ant or the most advanced Guru.

You are all the forms of life, but simultaneously you are a personification of the Deity within your limited physical shape. But it is precisely your physical shape that separates you from your innate divinity. This shape has been imparted to you temporarily in order to enable you to test yourselves in earthly life during many millions of years, coming through thousands and thousands of embodiments on Earth.

You have been using this shape for the purposes set up by God. God wishes to manifest Himself through your physical shape. Your task is to give God an opportunity to be manifested through you.

You have to bend yourselves to God who you are in reality. This is the task of every man. You must take care of your shape, keep it fit, and nourish it with all the necessary elements.

Nevertheless, you must never forget that you are God; therefore, you cannot do things unworthy of God.

Look back at your life and at its circumstances. Do they correspond to the Divine pattern?

19

You have to pay attention to all the aspects of your life. What do you eat? What do you wear? Whom do you communicate with? How do you treat your relations and friends?

They are also Gods in the physical shape. And your attitude to them must be similar to your attitude to God. You can attend a temple or a church. You see icons there. You worship these Gods. But there is no big difference between you and the people surrounding you and Gods in the temple. All of us represent manifestations of the Deity.

Yes, all of us are at different levels of manifestation of the Deity, but it does not make a big difference.

Do agree that if you treat yourself as God and if you treat the people around you as Gods, your life will change. The longer you are able to keep the image of the Deity in your consciousness, the sooner your life will change.

That is why it is necessary for you to have a representation of God at home or at your work place.

It is very important for you to have a model for imitation before your eyes. Since your world is a world of shapes, it is very important for you to continuously visualize God before you, knowing that you are indivisible with Him.

Do you agree with me? You gradually become one and indivisible with the images that you are keeping in your consciousness and to which you are aspiring.

Look at everything surrounding you at home, in the street. Pay attention to those images that you are staring at when looking at advertisements filling up your TV programs. Do you think all this resembles the Divine reality?

I offer you the cheapest way to become God. You simply have to guard yourself against imperfect images and to surround yourself with perfect Divine images. It does not matter to which religion or faith these images belong.

These must be images raising your consciousness and enabling you to dwell in a more perfect state of consciousness and maximizing your approximation to the perfect Divine vibrations as much as possible.

I am Shiva. I seldom come through people who do not adhere to the Hindu beliefs. People in the West cannot respect and treat God correctly.

That is why I advise you to learn the traditions of India as the country that managed to save the traditions of respect for God and in which the people who spend their lives in service to God are highly appreciated.

There is no other country in the world with such conditions for the service to God as in Mother India.

I love the people of this country and I aspire to dwell in the people of India.

If Russia manages to create a correct attitude to the moral upbringing and to God, it will be happiness for this country. Russia is a country loved by God. The future of

Russia is connected with the restoration of the traditions of the true faith — the faith based not on the external manifestations of respect but on the inner respect for God dwelling in every man.

At present the foremost task is to bring up the new generation in the tradition of respect for the older generation and for God dwelling in every man.

Any external image of God is necessary for you just to remind you about your Divine nature and about the Divine nature of the people surrounding you.

The respect for God has nothing in common with religion. Religion represents an external path that is necessary on a certain level, but you should not pay too much attention to this path.

In India there are many temples where people serve Gods. But there are also many wise men and yoga teachers in this country who teach people to respect the Deity in their hearts and who show them how to obtain a direct communion with the One within themselves and with gods who are always ready for it.

I promise to come to each of you who appeals to me in your heart. I will come and help you to resolve the most urgent problem that delays your spiritual evolution.

I AM Shiva, and I have been happy to communicate with you today.

Every effort of yours will be multiplied unprecedentedly because that is the call of the time and such is the situation on the planet now

November 27, 2005

I AM Shiva. I have come for the instructions concerning the interactions between different spiritual groups and schools that exist at the given historical moment.

We clearly see the whole narrow-mindedness of people's consciousness and all the reluctance of most people inhabiting planet Earth today to look at the Divine Truth and to accept it.

However, the efforts that are being applied by you are truly invaluable. Everyone who is awakened and capable of accepting the Divine Truth, even if not in its entire fullness, and everyone who aspires to accept this Truth is a priceless conductor for us, a crystal embryo through which we are able to introduce the elements of the new consciousness and the new relationships onto Earth.

23

Therefore, accept my gratitude to all those who aspire, to all those who make any — even the most minor — contribution to the common cause of saving planet Earth.

You may keep the aspiration in your heart and act according to this aspiration in your daily life; you may do the work that your consciousness is ready for; you may bring any material or spiritual gift to the altar of serving the Divine Truth. All your gifts will be accepted by us with gratitude and multiplied in our hearts.

The time has come when any — even the slightest — action of yours directed at maintaining the Divine vibration in your physical octave will be received, saved, and multiplied by us.

Blessed are your efforts, blessed are your aspirations, no matter in what area they would occur.

You cannot sit around doing nothing while in the physical octave; you can't not act because that is the call of the time and such is the will of God now.

Save and multiply your Divinity, your spiritual principle, and introduce the worship of God, the Higher Law existing in this Universe into your life.

Every effort of yours will be multiplied unprecedentedly because that is the call of the time and such is the situation on the planet now.

But for those who, for some reason, do not wish to obey the call of the time and the Higher Law, a hard time is coming because any counteraction that you are exerting will turn against you. And your actions will almost instantly bring the effects of your actions, which will be multiplied as well. And it will be impossible for you not to see the futility of your attempts to cling to the old consciousness, the old behavior, and the old way of thinking and acting.

Everything around you is subject to change, and it is already changing. Only the blind and the deaf can continue pretending that nothing is changing and everything is still the same.

No, I assure you, never ever have the changes on planet Earth been as rapid as they are in your time. And you can only adapt to these changes by changing yourself, by changing your consciousness, and by changing the stereotypes of your thinking and your behavior.

And now I wish to give you one more very important direction and instruction. Take it as a recommendation for your daily spiritual work.

Every day, starting from today and up to the New Year, I am asking you to spare at least several minutes a day to meditation, inner contemplation, and acceptance of the future image of your country and your planet.

You may draw the most daring images and plans in your consciousness, and you may use all of your imagination for that. The only condition is purity of your motives, your thoughts, and your aspirations. And I promise you, no matter what daring hopes, images, or plans you bear in your consciousness for the near future, for the next year, or the next few years, all of them will be supported by me personally, multiplied and returned to your world in the form of the Divine opportunity, the Divine mercy, and the Divine vision.

So, do dare to create the most daring plans. If they are in accordance with God's direction specific for the time of changes that planet Earth is experiencing, everything will be supported and manifested in your physical world.

You have very little time for your meditations — only until the end of this year.[3]

Do not forget to call upon me, Lord Shiva, before your meditations so that I can destroy everything old and obsolete that is lying in the way of manifesting your plans and give you the Divine opportunity and grant you my Love, Hope, and Faith.

Multiply your aspirations. Dare. Always remember that thought is material, and it is always capable of creating. And this creative ability of your thought, which is always inherent to you, will simply be strengthened many times during the period of time remaining until the New Year.

---

[3] Despite the fact that this opportunity, given by Lord Shiva, was active until the end of 2005, you should always remember that thought is material, and if it corresponds to the Will of God, the support of Heavens is soon to follow.
See the explanation of this dictation, given in the Message of Lord Shiva "Use the help, which Heavens give you, and do not disregard this help", dated March 13, 2006, page 60. (T.N. Mickushina)

Do not miss your chance and do not forget to write down all your thoughts, plans, and wishes on a separate sheet of paper. Meditate and detail your plan during each meditation. And when the New Year comes and during the next few years, observe what will be happening in your life and in the reality around you. And each of you will be granted a chance to face and realize the power of your thought when it gets in the unison with the Divine purposes and tasks for the given historical moment.

And now I am wishing you fruitful work and leaving you alone with your thoughts and ideas.

I AM Shiva and I have been with you today.

You have come to this world to learn a lesson of distinction

January 1, 2006

I AM Shiva, and I have come to you again through my Messenger.

For the topic of our conversation today, I would like to use a well-known parable about a horse: You can lead a horse to water but you cannot make it drink.

Our conversations sometimes resemble this parable. We lead you to the river of the Divine energy and give you a chance to obtain priceless knowledge, the wisdom of ages that is contained in our Messages. However, you and only you can make a decision and start drinking. Nobody can do it for you. And exactly the same way, our Messenger cannot force anyone to take the nectar of the Divine energy contained in our Messages.

Wise people do not hurry to touch the information that comes from an unfamiliar source. And this is right. If you absorb everything indiscriminately, you may get indigestion in your brain. You should very efficiently

29

select that information, which deserves your attention, in the reality surrounding you and separate it from the garbage that is located on the shelves of your stores and in the Internet in excess supply.

Not a long time ago, each book that we gave through our Messengers represented a wonder and was perceived as something incomprehensible and confusing. But now the time has changed, and a lot of such confusing information and literature has been spread around.

The problem is not in obtaining new information anymore; the problem is in protecting yourself against the flow of information that, with all its seeming novelty, presents poison in a beautiful package.

But, unlike the poison that you buy to get rid of pests, which clearly states on the packaging that it is a poison, it is not written on the covers of your books that they represent any kind of threat to your consciousness.

Therefore, we are changing our tactics. And from this moment our task is not to simply give you the information but to give you the knowledge on how to distinguish between the genuine information and the false one in the sea of information around you.

You know that there are no distinct criteria. And always, when it comes to distinction we suggest that you enter your heart and entrust your Higher Self with making a choice and evaluation. Your Higher Self always knows the Truth. However, the thought of the necessity to appeal to your Higher Self doesn't always come to your mind. Not to mention the fact that the purity of your lower bodies can be insufficient in order to feel and distinguish the voice of your Higher Self. That is why it will be appropriate to present external criteria on the basis of which you will be able to make a distinction in the flow of information surrounding you.

First, pay attention not to the quality of the binding or the cover of a book but primarily to the quality of the presentation of the material. And if the information is not given at the level understandable to you, then stop reading.

The fact of the matter is that there are many levels of presentation of information. And what is accessible to the consciousness of one cannot be accessible to the consciousness of another.

There is not always truth behind complex text.

However, if you have achieved a high degree of initiations, then you will always find on the shelves of the shops those keys that will allow you to recognize the Truth in the most intricate text.

We have intentionally resorted to making our Messages complex before. In that case we tried to scare away from us those who attempt to use our information for their selfish purposes. Now we are not inclined to complication. It is always possible to make the given information more complicated, but the essence of the given information is very simple, and as a rule, it is understandable even to a child. Therefore, no matter how long you would wander through the wilds of the so-called esoteric literature, we advise you to look up over the essence of what is given and answer a simple question on how the things that you read help you in your real life.

Does that information that you receive help you free yourself from the unreal part of yourself and strive for the eternal, everlasting reality? What does the information that you read give for the development of your soul? How does this information help you in your life?

You can obtain pieces of advice concerning many very skillful practices, but these practices lead you either to the multiplication of the illusion surrounding you or lead you away from your predestination and create the illusion that you are a very significant being on the cosmic scale.

In both cases you lose the point of support in your consciousness. You either go deeper into matter or soar in sky-high heights. As a result, the common thing is that you only generate illusion and create this illusion either on the physical plane or on the astral plane.

Your task is to constantly maintain the real viewpoint on your position in this world. And your real position is to stand with your feet firmly on Earth and at the same time to remember your cosmic origin and aspire to God.

The aspiration to God should not be confused with the desire to occupy a high position in the Cosmic Hierarchy.

Yes, it is possible that within many of you there are Higher Cosmic Beings who have come to Earth and are using every opportunity to help the civilizations of Earth. However, you should never forget that your soul is going through Earth's evolution. And that evolution is very gradual. Therefore, you cannot become a Great Cosmic Being during one lifetime. You can offer a Higher Cosmic Being to act through you, but it is more often that you give an opportunity to an astral plane being to act through you.

What is the criterion? How can one understand and make a distinction?

You know that in order for the Higher Cosmic Beings to act through you, you must say goodbye to most of your ego and undertake devoted service to the Cosmic Hierarchy.

In order to give yourself away as a slave to a being of the astral plane, none of your achievements are required at all, except for the desire of your ego to exalt itself.

Having read various kinds of superficial literature, many people consider themselves great beings who occupy a high position in the Cosmic Hierarchy.

These people have been playing their games for so long that they are already incapable of making a distinction. Moreover, they do not even worry about making any distinction because they are confident in their exclusiveness and greatness.

However, after several minutes of a conversation, it already becomes clear to people around whom they are dealing with. Therefore, we are asking you to develop the gift of distinction within yourselves. That is why we are telling you first and foremost to get rid of your ego. For your ego obstructs your distinction, your vision, and your service.

We feel sorry for those individuals who have gone along the path of self-exaltation. However, it is their choice. And they have made the choice they wanted to make. Your world of illusion is different due to the fact that everyone gets what they strive for. And if you want to become a Higher Cosmic Being, you will definitely become one. And you will receive all the signs from the subtle plane that you are in fact this Higher Cosmic Being. The whole problem is that your motive was wrong from the very beginning. You desired to become a powerful being.

The true motive would be to become the most humble being, the servant to all beings living on Earth. The true motive would be to liberate yourself from the ego and help all living beings.

Therefore, it is not even necessary for you to turn to other people for the confirmation of your, as you think, cosmic achievements. You simply need to answer the question what your motive was when you started studying esoteric literature. Did you desire to get something for yourself, or did you wish to give everything for serving life?

The Divine science seems to be very simple at first sight, but many go so deep into labyrinths of false concepts and knowledge that it becomes problematic for them to receive our very help.

Therefore, here is my advice to you: Before going deep into any teaching or following any practice or an external teacher, always analyze attentively the motive that drives you. For you will be attracted according to your vibrations and inner desires that are driving you to that group of people and to that teacher who will simply supply you with that which is necessary for you in order to achieve your goals. And never blame anyone outside of you that you have gotten into a cult or under someone's influence. For you and only you yourselves are responsible for everything that happens to you.

You have come to this world in order to get a lesson of distinction between the Good and the Evil, the illusion and the reality.

Learn your lessons by yourselves. And remember that we can help you only when you ask us for help.

I AM Shiva, and I have come to give some very important instructions.

We are looking for those who, in their consciousness, are able to go beyond the limits of the surrounding illusion

January 5, 2006

I AM Shiva, and I have come to you again through my Messenger.

Keep up your care about peace in your hearts. Consider the meaning of this phrase. This phrase is telling you about the peace or serenity within your hearts; this phrase is also telling you about caring for everything around you. Actually, everything that surrounds you depends on what is happening within you. Your dependence on your inner state is absolute. There is nothing outside of you that can leave a trace on your inner condition if you reach perfection in controlling your thoughts and feelings.

What a big difference in levels of consciousness there is on Earth. You know that what I mentioned above makes no sense at all for many people living on planet Earth. The deep information that is contained in these phrases goes past their consciousness without leaving any trace.

Why? That is because the level of their consciousness and the level of their vibrations do not give them the opportunity to catch the meaning of these words. Only those people whose vibrations are at the highest level possible in your octave are able to respond to these words and be inspired by their meaning.

Actually, everything around you represents a great illusion that is supported and exists only due to your consciousness, only due to your staying in your world and your interest in what is around you. Your energy flows where your attention is directed. Your energy flows toward what you are thinking about, what you are interested in.

Imagine that all people simultaneously lost their interest in the surrounding reality. All of you would simultaneously lose the desire to possess things of your world and own these things. You would lose interest in getting pleasures of your world. It does not mean that you would lose the meaning of your existence. The meaning of your existence would simply shift to other octaves, finer and more subtle.

What would happen to the world surrounding you in this case?

This world would cease existing and would gradually dissolve as a mirage.

I AM Shiva. I come to you because one of the functions that I perform in this Universe is contracting the worlds. I am the destroyer of the illusion. I control the process of contraction of the illusion.

The moment has come when your consciousness must be expanded and face the reality so that the illusion can cease to exist.

You think that my visits to you and my talks with you through my Messenger are accidental. No, it is just that the moment has come when in the beginning, a small number of incarnated individuals and later, more and more people will be able to perceive this new information that we give.

Your world is similar to a big pile of firewood. It is enough to bring a match and light up a few dry logs, and then the entire pile will be on fire. Now we are searching for those of you who are able to burn. It is because not all the logs are ready. Lots of them are still wet. But when more and more people are able to perceive our vibrations and the new information that we are giving, your whole world will be taken over by fire, and there will not be any trace left from your illusory world. This process will not take much time in terms of cosmic measures.

Therefore, we are searching for those among you who are able to carry the flame, the Light, the energy, and our vibrations.

That is why we are saying that those who, with their consciousness, still continue holding on to the surrounding world belong to the past.

There are always people who prefer the Old due to their conservative thinking and the backwardness of their consciousness. And there are always people who look forward to the New. We are looking for such people. We are looking for those among you who are able to perceive the new thinking and the new consciousness. We are looking for those whose consciousness is able to go beyond the limits of the surrounding illusion.

Go up high, toward the Higher worlds — the celestial worlds.

Leave the limited world of your native planet and fly out of your nest into the expanse of the Universe.

We are searching for the brave and the striving, the ones who are not afraid of the new and the unknown.

Who among you are able to step into the unknown mystery? You know that only those people who in their consciousness are able to overcome the limitations of the three-dimensional world surrounding you, can advance to learn about the Higher Worlds.

Life does not end. Life is infinite. Life just shifts into new forms.

This process is similar to perpetual motion, an infinite spiral that never ceases and never stops.

Only the one who has never gone through a winter cannot believe that after winter, spring will come and then summer.

Now your existence on planet Earth resembles existence in the conditions of a very severe winter that you have generated with your consciousness.

You have to understand that this state of yours is temporary. It will change.

That is why we are calling you to change your consciousness, to be ready for a change, and to aspire to Higher states.

It does not mean that you will lose those joys that you are used to receiving from life around you. Your perception will just gain refinement. Pleasures that you will be able to experience will surpass all your expectations. It is because none of earthly pleasures can be compared to those pleasures that you are able to experience in the finer worlds.

The gradual changes in your consciousness are the guarantee of the fact that the difficult stage that your civilization is currently experiencing will be surmounted as smoothly as possible.

But you know that if a baby bird does not hurry to leave the nest, then the careful mother pushes it to the new life, to find the freedom of flight. To gain this new life it is necessary to take the first step and come out of the limits of your human consciousness and learn to think in categories that are not connected with your world and the limitations of your world.

I AM Shiva. I have come to teach you how to destroy the illusion in your consciousness.

Use the help that Heavens give you, and do not disregard this help

March 13, 2006

I AM Shiva, having come again through my Messenger. The state of affairs is that I have come to give the next Message that will allow you to understand the situation and to make clear those guidelines for yourself that you may choose to follow in your lives.

As soon as the previous cycle of the Dictations was over, we had a sense of great relief that, using the incarnated conductor, we managed the realization of the plan and gave the information that humankind needed.

However, we then encountered absolutely unpredictable resistance to our actions. That resistance passed through many incarnated people's minds, and many of them consider themselves light-bearers. Therefore, I have come to assure you once again that we will continue giving our Messages, no matter what efforts it will cost us. And we will do that according to our plans and our terms that come as provided by space opportunities and a necessity.

Therefore, I have come today to give you an understanding once again that no matter how the situation is developing on planet Earth, we, the Ascended Masters, will work with mankind of Earth and will continue our attempts to change humanity's consciousness.

It seems that there is very little information in our Messages, though each time we keep wondering how the people are found who are ready to respond to all of our propositions and remarks at our first summons and do those things that are necessary now.

You know that one of the most important things that humanity faces is the change of consciousness. And thus, everything that favors the change of earthling's consciousness is good. Of course, we mean the change of consciousness that we try to manifest in your octave, but not the change of consciousness that you think should take place.

Therefore, all the ways of spreading the knowledge contained in the given Dictations are good. Also good are the ways of communicating the information to people, including private meetings, training classes, seminars, organization of schools for parents and children to learn the foundations of the Law of Karma and the principles of behavior, based on the Divine Law.

All that is genuinely from God needs your help to grow and widen.

Therefore, when you are surprised that not everything around you looks like you would like it to be, we say: "So much the better! You have seen where to apply your efforts, your abilities and your talents!"

Look around and analyze thoroughly what you personally can change and what you think should be changed, relying on your opportunities and your abilities.

Once again I would like to remind you of the Dictation that I gave last year on the 27th of November.[4] As soon as you turn your thoughts in the necessary direction and imbue the images emerging in your mind with the Divine energy, I will have the opportunity to help you and to imbue your imageries with my energy.

There is a Divine opportunity that is given for the planet at a certain moment. That opportunity is being given now through our Messenger. Sometimes nothing is required from you but the acceptance of our Messenger. And as soon as you recognize the Messenger of the Hierarchy, you automatically stand on the steps of the Hierarchy. And all the Hierarchy has an opportunity to help you in your affairs and in the realization of your plans.

I would also like to stop at one important moment. Our Messenger is the person who keeps our vibrations, constantly carrying her devotion to the Hierarchy through all living situations and realizing our plans on Earth. For you who are in incarnation, our Messenger is the incarnated master, the Guru. And that means that you

---

[4] "Every effort of yours will be multiplied unprecedentedly because that is the call of the time and such is the situation on the planet now." Shiva, November 27, 2005.

44

must follow the instructions that you receive from our Guru as if I gave you those instructions personally.

Here you will need all your distinction to understand to what degree you can trust the external Guru and to what degree you should be guided by those instructions that you receive from your heart, from your Higher Self.

The Teaching about Guru requires additional deciphering. I think that to some extent we will be able to give that Teaching of ours for you because there are too many of those who consider themselves a guru or pretend to be a guru, but all of them — or almost every one of them — do not have the main attribute of the true Guru: the ability of self-sacrifice and the ability to sacrifice their entire selves on the altar of service.

Therefore, no matter how your human conscious-ness impedes your understanding of the true significance of the Guru's mantle and the Guru-chela relationship, any obstacle that is within you can and should be swept away with the help of your sincere aspiration and your devotion to the Hierarchy.

Every time that you need to receive validations or refutations of the verity or falsity of any person pretending to be your Guru or our Messenger, please apply to me for help.

Just take the image of me in your hands or come up to my image in the form of a statue and sincerely ask me for help.

As soon as I see your sincerity and aspiration, I will certainly help you. And you will get that distinction, which you need at the current stage of your development.

Therefore, use the help that Heavens give you, and do not disregard this help.

I AM Shiva, and I am saying goodbye to you today, but I hope for new meetings.

We invite you to establish a new type of relations between the Guru and a chela

March 15, 2006

I AM Shiva, coming to you again to talk about the Path you will follow if you choose the Path that we are teaching you about through our Messenger.

There are many ways and many roads in your material world. Unfortunately, most of those ways and roads lead nowhere. Incarnation by incarnation you wander about the illusion and cannot find the true Path.

And even when at last you discover the Truth on your Path, you begin to doubt whether what you face comes from God or not.

It often happens that you choose the right Way and already follow it, but at some moment of weakness in your heart, you fall under the influence of your carnal mind and begin to doubt. Your doubts are produced by your imperfection. Therefore, when you choose the Path to follow or start doubting the Path that you are following, you should always consider this: Where do your doubts come from?

Are your doubts reasonable or are they just a result of your fear and your lack of self-confidence?

You should constantly distinguish your inner states. Are you influenced by unreal forces or do you just reasonably analyze the Path that you follow?

Every time you analyze your inner work, you have to be guided only by your intuition and the voice of your heart.

That is why we tirelessly repeat to you: "Develop your intuition, your distinction, and your connection with the real world of God."

It is hard for you to do this when you are completely sunk in the illusion. Therefore, we send our Messengers and our servants who show you the Path and help you to orientate yourself in the sea of life.

However, you and only you can choose whom to follow and whose recommendations to be guided by.

The situation is complicated by the fact that however devoted and sincere our Messenger is, she took a human incarnation, and along with the incarnation she had to take a part of the world's karma, a burden that allows her to stay in the incarnation.

Seeing the imperfection of our Messengers, you can be puzzled and seized with additional doubts.

Therefore, we tell you that you should not blindly trust those people who proclaim themselves as messiahs, messengers, and teachers. There is always an element of unpredictability in any situation, and that person who was our rightful representative and who carried our mantles not long ago, can make a mistake and even stray from the Path. So you should carefully watch and analyze all the actions of our Messengers and be able to distinguish between accidental mistakes in their actions, which are impossible to avoid in your world, and a more serious sin of betrayal and deviation from the principles of the Brotherhood.

This Teaching is new, and we dare give it now through our Messenger with a hope that many of you have achieved the level of development that will allow you not to make categorical judgments and refuse to follow our Messengers at all.

No, now it is not the right time for you to follow the Path and choose the Path on your own. You cannot do so without our representatives and our Messengers. But you have to approach your choice of people whose advice you decide to listen to and whose guidance you decide to follow consciously, along with the measures of your inner consonance and your distinction.

If in former times unconditional obedience and strict following the Guru's guidance was demanded of you, now we tell you that you should listen to your inner voice and your inner intuition about everything, and only after that you can follow the outer instructions of any Guru.

The people who are not ready for such new Guru-chela relations will not be able to follow the

49

Teachings being given by us through this Messenger. They need other harder instructions and abidance with outer dogmas and rules. That is why we give this Teaching, but we completely understand that different human individuals are at various stages of their development, and what is good for one might be undesirable and premature for another.

It is well known that if a person had a long stay underground and did not have access to daylight, an instantaneous exposure to bright sunlight can totally blind him and do irreparable harm to his health.

People incarnated on planet Earth have different levels of consciousness; and now we are giving our Teachings for those who are ready to be in the vanguard, for those who are ahead of their brothers and who are ready to start immediate relations with the Ascended Masters, based on cooperation and mutual respect. However, while you are incarnated, the principle of unconditional obedience to the Ascended Masters and our representatives is fundamental for you.

But, you make the decision about such obedience in your heart by yourself, and you should always be ready to change your decision if you feel that the circumstances have changed.

Therefore, Guru-chela relations typical for the new era will be notable for you to have creative, mutually-enriching relations with your Guru, rather than the relations based on compulsion and diktat as had been accepted before in many of our organizations.

And those relations are more suitable for the spirit of the time and those common democratic reforms that are taking place in the world.

Let me repeat once again that not all people will be able to establish and accept the new relations. And many people are just not ready for establishing such relations because any hint that the teacher can be wrong is a signal for them not to consider their Guru's opinion at all.

We invite you to establish a new type of relations between the Guru and a chela, the relations based on unconditional love, true brotherhood, and cooperation.

We hope that a sufficient number of individuals, who are ready for such relations and already follow them, will be found.

I am glad to give you this important Teaching today, which you undoubtedly need.

I AM Shiva, and I have been with you today!

A Teaching on the Path of Apprenticeship

April 22, 2006

I AM Shiva, having come to you again!

I have come, and as always, I have come to give you the information that you need and that your outer consciousness and your subtle bodies need.

There have been a number of important events since our previous communication. The result of those events can be briefly described as Heaven's approval of the current situation on Earth. And if earlier, during the days of the winter solstice when we were giving the previous cycle of the Dictations, we expressed our displeasure with the situation on Earth, now we cannot stop repeating that the Heavens express their approval and joy due to the changes that are occurring on Earth.

The situation is changing, and if it is still not noticed by the majority of humanity, those who can feel higher energies notice the changes and follow these changes in their consciousness.

As it was at our last meeting, I have come to give a short Teaching concerning the Path of Apprenticeship. The vital need for this Teaching becomes more and more obvious. As soon as humankind of Earth is carried away

by the illusion, the connection with the Hierarchy and our Teaching, which we have been giving for many centuries through different incarnated Teachers and Messengers, becomes lost.

So, every time we have to restore our connection again and again through the conductor that we get in the dense world. At this moment we are talking about our Messenger, Tatyana. You see that we continue using this conductor. We are proceeding with our work because when getting a worthy conductor, we try to use it at full capacity. We do not take into account the state of the person's physical body or her inner state. Nothing can stop us when it is necessary to transmit information and the Law for its application in the physical world.

Having this conductor, we will try to use it not only for the transmission of our Messages but also for creating our outpost, the base, the foundation, and the focus of Light on the physical plane. When we get something on the physical plane that can allow us to fix our focus of Light, we will transmit our information and will influence the raising of the vibrations of many, using the bodies of the Messenger. This is similar to the process that happens when you throw a stone in the quiet water of a pond: The waves from the thrown stone spread around the whole pond. Everything that has gotten into the scope of that spreading wave starts to feel the vibrations.

Therefore, the transfer of knowledge is not always connected with giving information through the Word. There is a certain law that allows the transfer of information from the aura of a Teacher to the aura of a disciple. In order to do that, Guru-chela relations based on complete unconditional Love and cooperation should be established. At the moment when the auras of a Teacher and a disciple touch, the momentum of the Teacher's achievements goes to the disciples on that complete and unconditional feeling of Love.

We try to create the conditions in which we could use the potential of our Messenger at full capacity, not only giving information through her in the form of the Word, but also giving the information to our chelas through her conductors to accelerate their development.

All we need is to create very comfortable conditions in any place on planet Earth where people can come and stay for some period of time. You can call it an ashram, a community, or a training center. But the purpose of that place is to serve as a focus on the physical plane where we can fix our energies and transmit our vibrations. The only requirements for this place on our part are its maximum distance from any populated areas and the absence of any places where there are people who do not have a significant level of vibrations so as not to create the state of premature testing in those people. Every person who gets into the sphere of our focus of Light experiences the rising of vibrations. And you know that as soon as you get an additional portion of Light, that Light starts to intensively push out any manifestations of imperfections from your aura. So, the person who is not ready, who has not started Guru-chela relations with our Messenger, will feel different uncomfortable states, which will cause increased tension.

Therefore, the more isolated, quiet, and comfortable the place of our future focus is, the better results we will be able to achieve. I appeal to those who have information about such places at their disposal: Where is it possible to organize our ashram? Would you mind telling our Messenger about that or applying to me personally with your letter?

This is a very important step. In order to make our place safe, to a certain extent, from negative influences and any property arguments, I have informed our Messenger about the conditions on which that ashram ought to exist.

I repeat once again that there is a certain Law according to which we perform our work on the physical plane. And that Law assumes the presence of disciples in the Teacher's aura in order to accelerate the process of advancement along the Path.

Those of you who have attended our events that we have carried out together with our Messenger could feel how the process of changing your consciousness has accelerated after those events.

We will continue holding our events. I think that all of you who wish that those events should continue will be able to visit them in due time.

In the near future Tatyana will have to carry the additional responsibility of creating and fixing our focus of Light. Therefore, I ask you to give her all the necessary help and support no matter what kind of help or support it is. Sometimes it is enough just to express your mental support, to send your Love and gratitude for service. And the impulse of your heart can neutralize the impact of a huge amount of negative energy that is drawn to our Messenger automatically because she is on top of the peak, and all winds and hurricanes hit her first.

I have told everything I have planned to tell during today's talk. I hope that I can count on you and your help in our work.

I AM Shiva.

I offer you this method in the hope that you will be able to use it in your everyday spiritual work

July 3, 2006

I AM Shiva, having come again!

I AM Shiva, I have come!

I have come and I am glad to meet you through my Messenger again!

Since we finished the spring cycle of the Dictations, several important events in the finer world have taken place, and the most important among them is that humankind of Earth have started to give in to the efforts we tirelessly applied and to move along the evolutionary Path that was planned. Some time ago, none of the Ascended Masters was sure that it would be possible to carry out the forthcoming transformations on Earth. Now with certainty, we can state the fact that we have managed to do everything so that humankind can return to the evolutionary Path of development and harmonize a part of the distorted energies of the past. Now we should not slow down the pace. Therefore, I have come in order to direct you to your further deeds and provide instructions to those who are capable of perceiving them.

The main and most important thing for humankind now is harmonization. By harmonization I mean a combination of measures and methods that will lead to the levelling of consciousness development rates in different regions of Earth, in different countries and continents. You know that our Messages are spread very successfully in Eurasia. But there are other continents. There, people know very little about our Messages and the new Teaching that we are giving. Therefore, there are two ways to harmonize the situation on the planet. The first way assumes intensive spreading of our Messages to other continents, especially in America. The second way is simpler and at the same time more difficult because it requires of you a particular degree of selflessness and certain spiritual achievements. That way assumes particular spiritual work to be done on the finer plane. Now I will explain to you what it exactly means.

Every time you read our Messages, imagine the people of those continents where our Messages are not accessible so far. Imagine Africa, America, and Australia. And every time visualize that you communicate with the representatives of those countries and give them a notion about the Teaching that we give you in the Dictations. If there are people among your acquaintances who live on those continents, then please, do visualize those people and tell them in your mind about the knowledge you have received, and have a mental talk with them. Try to explain to them, in your words, the foundations of the Teaching you have received. Thus, the goal will be achieved, and our energy of changes will touch the consciousness of the people who live on those continents, and the desire will rise in them to read our Messages and to assimilate the information contained in them. Even if those people's external consciousness does not respond to the work you do, their fine bodies will receive the impression necessary for the changes. And again the foundation of the changes will be laid by you together with us.

I am giving you this method, and you can use it for working with the people who have a big influence in the countries where they live. They can be outstanding statesmen, artists, and science and culture representatives. Your consciousness will give you a hint with whom and how you can work. I am offering you this method in the hope that you will be able to use it in your everyday spiritual work. Before you start your visualizations, please do take care about your harmonious state of consciousness so that none of your small everyday home cares can worry you. Take care of the purity of your inner space, for you will transfer your inner state to the people with whom you will be working distantly.

The purer your thoughts are and the more elevated your state is, then the more wonderful results you will achieve.

I have to warn you of another important moment. If your state is not harmonious and your motives are not pure, the energy that you will put into your work can create your karma, which you will have to work off yourself later. Always remember that karma is created not only by your actions and deeds but also by your thoughts and feelings. Therefore, I turn to you now in the hope that you have already read all the Dictations we have been giving through our Messenger, and your consciousness is completely prepared for this important work we are asking you for.

I am talking to you as to equal beings capable of understanding our problems and of sacrificing small everyday interests for the Common Good, for the prosperity of your mother planet.

Always remember that there are no enemies on your planet; there are only people in poor states of consciousness, including ignorance.

Ignorance and lack of knowledge are the enemies you will have to fight with. Therefore, bring the Light of knowledge to the people of planet Earth. Come up, kindle your torches, and bring the Light to those who need it.

Exactly the same principle can be laid as the foundation of your work with your relatives who need knowledge but for some reason are not ready to apply their own efforts to receive it. Do help them. Tell them about the Teaching. Tell them about it in your mind when you are in a good and harmonious inner state. This particularly concerns your closest relatives with whom you have karmic connections. Try to give them the knowledge at the level of thoughts and feelings. Do not hesitate to send Love to your closest ones. For nothing is as favorable for people's souls as watering them with the energy of Love from your hearts every day.

I was glad to meet you again today. And I hope that this meeting and my talk have been useful for you. I wish you success on your Path!

I AM Shiva, always with you!

A talk about God

January 2, 2007

I AM Shiva, having come again in order to give you the next Message!

Shiva I AM!

I have come to pay my visit exactly at the beginning of the year when many of you are concentrating on future plans and are surprised watching how your lives and everything around you are changing. I have come to give you direction for your inner work and for your outer work again.

Your inner work of self-perfection always means only the realization of yourself as the Divine manifestation and giving up everything within you that is not of the Divine.

Every time you try to find within you something that is unreal and put this quality on a pedestal instead of the Divinity, it is called going astray from the Path. And you should thoroughly watch all such moments.

In your life you will encounter the worshipping of your relatives, your spouses, your children, people whom you love. In your life you will encounter the worshipping of things, such as luxuries and money. You will encounter the worshipping of power and force. You will put much on the pedestal and worship this fetish like God.

However, much time will pass, and you will start realizing that there is nothing that can take the place of the true Divinity in your heart.

Some of you have already started realizing this simple truth. And as too many deities were thrown down from their pedestals by you or by life circumstances, you are afraid of losing your attachment to something once again. Therefore, many of you approach with suspicion the true God residing in your hearts and trying to establish contact with you.

Do not be afraid. The time has come at last when you are supposed to meet the real manifestation of Divinity. You are supposed to meet God within you. And this takes place only when you throw down from the pedestal one false idol after another.

Do not be afraid. There is always a criterion that will help you to distinguish the true God from many false gods and goddesses.

And you yourself always know when you face the true manifestation of Divinity in your life.

When you are calm, peaceful and filled with Divine tranquility in your heart, nobody in the world will be able to convince you that you have not found the true God.

It is impossible to take this for anything else. However, many of you still seek and find false gods and graven images.

How can you find one true God in your heart without losing your way?

The truth is that you cannot find true God until you reject false gods and any attachments to your world. If you try to find God in order to realize some desire or quality of yours, you will not be able to find true God. You will not be able to find true God until you aspire to Him with all your heart, until you give up every human aspiration, including the aspiration to worship God.

It is difficult for you to believe and understand this, but many people replace the true faith in God with blind worship of a deity.

The external worship of God has nothing in common with the inner worship of Divinity. And the external worship of God is just the first, the very first step on the way to true Divinity, being on the throne in your heart.

Each of you must come to God. Each of you will inevitably come to your God, being on the throne of your heart. However, each of you will look for many gods living in temples and churches, pagodas and mosques.

You will be looking for your God for a long time. And you will find Him one nice day when it seems to you that life is meaningless for you, when you are not attached to anything in your world any more. You will be back where you started your life, being at a loose end with your family, or your job, or anything else that was important for you and that has gone. And at that moment when there is nothing in your world to which you feel an attachment, at that moment you will turn your eyes toward the sky in your last hope, and you will say in your heart:

"Lord, help me, Lord. I know that You exist. I know that You hear me. I believe in Your Might and Your Mercy. I love You, Lord, and I believe that all You have done to me was necessary only for me to come to You. Lord, forgive me everything that I did through my foolishness. I thank You, Lord, for Your Teaching and for letting me go through all tests and coming out of them with credit. Lord, help me to find You and never part with You ever in my life."

At that moment, it will seem to you that the Heavens have opened. You will feel what you have never felt in your life. You will understand that everything you have aspired to, you already have and you always had. And all of this is within you, in your heart, but you did not want to see it and hear it up to this moment of your life when your ears started hearing and your eyes opened.

I BELIEVE and I HOPE that each of you either had or will have such an experience. And I hope that this experience will leave such an indelible mark on your soul that you will always stay in consonance with God until the end of this life of yours. And whatever difficult life situations you get into, you will not blame God and accuse Him of your misfortunes and troubles. You will understand and accept that you are the only one to blame for your misfortunes and troubles because you were full of pride and ignorance. And ignorance covered your eyes.

I am glad that our talk today has taken place. And I am glad that I could bring home to your consciousness that state which will enable you to overcome yourselves and rise to God.

I AM Shiva, the destroyer of the unreal in you.

A Teaching on the Transition

July 8, 2007

I AM Shiva, who has come to you again!

Shiva I AM!

I have come to you on this day! I have come!

I am happy today that I have the opportunity to speak through my Messenger again!

Each time I come in order to support the connection between our worlds and to continue your instruction. You know that now the time is coming when it is necessary to part with the illusions of your consciousness. You know that your victory over death is inevitable if only you are able to elevate your consciousness to the level of your immortal part.

You are like a matryoshka doll. Every time when you open another matryoshka, you see a new one. The same is the principle of your development. When you part with your physical body, you simply transition in your consciousness to a higher vibrational level. You will continue to come into incarnation and take on physical bodies until you learn how to constantly reside at a higher energy level.

Therefore, our task is to prompt your consciousness to transition to a higher energy level. This gradual process will simply accelerate now. You are slightly behind the cosmic deadlines, and that is why we have to hasten you.

You follow us for as long as you are able to change your consciousness. When you begin to understand many things better than we, as it seems to you, and prefer to explore new-fashioned teachings and practices, we do not interfere. It can be very amusing to observe how you fancy yourselves as very high cosmic beings. You think that you are great cosmic beings. However, before you actually become these great cosmic beings, you have to graduate from earthly school and consecutively pass through all the stages along the Path.

Therefore, when you are being called to the instant elevation of your consciousness and to transition to a different energy level, if I were you I would strongly question how realistic is what is being offered.

For millions of years we have been following the evolutionary development of mankind. In terms of comprehending the Divine Truth, your consciousness has not advanced very far in the past thousands of years. You should not confuse the development of your intellect with the development of the Divine consciousness. It is still very hard for you to comprehend the simple Divine Truths related to reincarnation and the Law of arma. It is a great difficulty for you to overcome a small attachment or an inconspicuous habit. This happens because the greatest difficulty is related to overcoming the attachment to the physical plane.

It seems strange when you are offered to instantly receive big initiations and achieve considerable advancement on the path. If I were you, I would think about at what expense this great advancement will take place. Who will give you the energy to transform your karmic loads? And on what terms do your benefactors engage in your fast advancement? Does it not resemble the sale of your soul, of your life energy, to the devil?

Try to understand how the Cosmic Law operates.

69

When, due to the Law of free will, you make your choices and lower your vibrations, you come down to the material world, deepening into the matter more and more. After that, you will need a great amount of energy, which must be equal to all the Divine energy that you have once misused. That energy must come to you under certain terms.

Imagine that a miracle has happened and all the energy that you had misused for millions of years has come back to you instantly. Considering the density of your physical body and your vibrations, how will you be able to withstand that energy? For your being, it will be similar to an explosion of a supernova. Your consciousness will not be able to instantly adjust to the new energy level. That is why we teach you a gradual evolutionary path. In the course of an accelerated evolution, almost all humanity would die. We do not have the desire to promote your death. We have the desire for you to continue your evolution at a higher energy level.

Think carefully and compare my words with many of the teachings and theories that you come across and that are related to an instant leap. Who will give the energy for that leap?

I am telling you this as a being that has been granted the power and called to contract the illusion. I am telling you that it is impossible to instantly transition to a level of consciousness of greater quality unless that transition is accompanied by the death of almost all human individuals inhabiting the planet Earth. We teach the evolutionary path and we give the knowledge, thanks to which you will be able to naturally elevate your consciousness to a higher energy level. In that way, a greater number of beings living on Earth will be able to continue the evolution. Any revolutionary change of vibrations can happen only when the efforts that we make are not successful in the near future.

We believe that the majority of you are ready to continue the evolution and to change the vibrations of your body to such an extent that you will survive in the new conditions. However, you should also make the efforts to extend the evolution and to not end up in unfavorable conditions that exist on the planets that had desired to separate themselves from God.

All that follows the Divine Law existing in this Universe must be provided with everything necessary for its evolutionary development. All that does not wish to follow the Divine Law will face greater and greater hardships until a complete termination of development occurs, and the angels of death will escort the remnants of the soul to repolarization.

You are given exactly as much as is needed to make a conscious choice of the path and to continue your evolution. We have not spoken so clearly and in such detail through any other Messenger of the past or the present.

I AM Shiva! I came today in order to provide your consciousness with important information for thinking over in the stillness of your heart and for making the decision.

I AM Shiva.

I have come to destroy all dogmas in your consciousness

January 5, 2008

I AM Shiva!

I have come!

It has been a long time since we had an opportunity to speak through our Messenger.

I am always at your service, but unfortunately, I am not honored much in your world. There are a few faithful acolytes and they live in my beloved India.

Among Western humanity, it is rare indeed to find people who are devoted to me and are able to perceive my energy and my vibrations.

My energies and vibrations are very hard for you to bear because I am continuous motion. I am fire, water, and air. I am in constant motion, in continuous dance.

I have been distracted, but perhaps we should start today's talk. I have given my state to you, and now you will be able to better perceive the information that I am going to give you.

We are happy that we can continue the work through our Messenger in Russia. I have always said that this country has an enormous and still-undisclosed spiritual potential.

Russia represents a bride given in marriage. Different spiritual teachings try to settle there, but the Teaching that has to come to Russia and should stay there has only now started taking root. The seed is still in the soil, and there are no sprouts.

However, the main process has started. The seed has been sown; the soil is fertilized and watered.

Now we can only wait for the sprouts of new consciousness in the Russian people.

We have carried out the enormous preparation work. We have destroyed the dogmas of old religions and saved Russia from the domination of different, doubtful, spiritual bridegrooms.

Russia, with all of its unpredictability, possesses innate scrupulousness and cleanliness. That is why we look forward to and carefully track all the processes that are going on in this country.

The new consciousness, the new spiritual Teaching, comes quietly and sensibly. It has already started revealing itself.

There won't be a famous person or an organization. The new spiritual Teaching will come through the hearts of people who live in this great country.

Beware of thinking that it is not the right time or that nothing is happening. All the main preparatory work processes are over on both the Higher and on the physical planes.

Hundreds and thousands of people have been prepared by us to adopt the new consciousness, the new thinking, the new Teaching in their hearts.

Cups are ready. We are seeking to fill every cup that is ready with as much energy as it can hold.

As soon as we fill the cups of these few, many other people will be able to touch our Teaching and have our Light, directly seeing us and communicating with us, the Ascended Masters.

We will be able to come closely to those places in Russia that are still free, clean, and are not inhabited. Russia is a rich country. We can make this country ten times and one hundred times richer as soon as our Teaching penetrates the consciousness of the critical proportion of the population of the country. The whole country will turn and stand motionless in the expectation of the miracle, and the miracle will happen because all people will know about it and will look for it.

This miracle of spiritual renewal and spiritual growth will appear as quickly as bamboo shoots out of the ground. You know that bamboo lies dormant underground for a long time growing its roots. But as soon as the time comes, the plant leaps up significantly, growing several meters in a few days.

That will happen to Russia. It's still dormant, keeping its virgin consciousness until the seed has sprouted up, the seed we sowed with the help of this Messenger and many others.

The only faith and the only Teaching that has ever existed on Earth is the Teaching that we, the Ascended Masters, have been giving to you. It had different names and trends, and the sense of our Teaching was distorted, but we always gave the same Teaching.

The time has come, and all of you have to rise above religious dogmas and limits that you have believed in for ages. You have to raise your consciousness so high that all the limits and barriers disappear from your consciousness. You have to ascend to the stage from which you can see the oneness of all the people of the planet and all the religions existing in the world.

The limitation of your consciousness constrains you.

I have come to destroy all dogmas in your consciousness and everything that prevents you from seeing the Face of God — not the face painted on the walls of the temples but in the starry sky and clouds.

I have come and destroyed everything I can destroy in your consciousness without breaking the rhythm of your lives.

There is much energy, and you cannot bear any more.

I have been with you today! I AM Shiva!

It is time to carry out the grandiose changes in your consciousness

December 27, 2008

I AM Shiva!

I have come!

I have come on this day to destroy some stereotypes in your consciousness that have firmly anchored there for the last thousands of years.

The main stereotype that I have come to destroy today concerns the fact that you yourselves can make decisions in your lives, and you are free to act the way you like. Yes, there is the Law of free will in your world. We cannot interfere in your decisions until the moment when your decisions, your behavior, and your way of living threaten the civilization that exists on your planet.

But the moment comes when your free will leads you into a karmic deadlock. Everything you do begets the bacchanalia of permissiveness, a feast during the plague.

This must be stopped. Now I have come in order to remind your souls of other times that were on Earth.

There was the supremacy of the Cosmic Law in those times. Mankind of Earth submitted to their preceptors who were standing at a higher stage of evolutionary development. The misuse of free will led to the fact that the veil became too dense, and the preceptors of mankind could not stay present among the people any longer.

The current period is called the Kali Yuga, the age of darkness and ignorance.

That is why we come now in order to say that your stay in the mode of ignorance is coming to an end. The time comes when your preceptors are to come back and walk among you. But for this you have to create the proper conditions on Earth. These conditions should come back to your world by means of changing your consciousness. When humanity persists and tries to defend the position of its ego, there comes a time of great disasters that sweep away entire cities and even continents.

Therefore, I am not trying to scare you, but I say that the time is short. Your humility before the Supreme Law is needed now more than ever.

Stop playing gods. Just be gods. Become equal among us, but for this you need to sacrifice something. You have to sacrifice your unreal part, your ego, which is used to running the show in the physical plane of planet Earth.

I am telling you: "The period of the Kali Yuga is coming to an end. It is time to carry out the grandiose changes in your consciousness."

You should establish humility before the Supreme Law.

Your ego makes you rush about, doubt, and search for something in order to satisfy its whims and desires.

You should understand that the life of the unreal part of you comes to an end. Hard times come to those individuals who are not willing to adapt to new conditions, who stick together with their unreal part. Your karma that you continue to create because of your thoughtlessness or ignorance exceeds all reasonable limits. Even all the might of the Ascended Hosts is not enough to hold your karma within certain limits so that it cannot overflow its banks and wipe out most of the continents.

I AM Shiva, the destroyer of illusion. My might cannot be compared to the might of all book sorcerers who considered themselves gods in the flesh.

Do come to your senses. In your age, when the Divine power descending into your being through the crystal cord is reasonably reduced, you cannot implement any serious actions and cause any significant opposition to the Divine might. You are only able to aggravate your karma and make it huge.

I come in order for you to understand that the resistance of your unreal part comes to an end.

There is still a short period of time when you are given the opportunity to change your view of evolution.

It is unreasonable, extremely unreasonable, to separate yourself from God and from the Divine Hierarchy that exists in the Universe. It seems that you have been told about this many times, and I am surprised to see that most of the information that we give is not mastered by you. You seize the top line but you do not move deeper into the given Teaching.

It seems so simple to be reconciled with the Supreme Law and to stop resisting, but your ego rises again and again and continues its struggle. Who are you struggling with?

Doesn't it seem strange to you that you are struggling against the true God and that you are fencing yourself from us by worshiping gods invented by you that you created in your own image?

Hasn't the time come to turn to the one God of this Universe and stop praying to gods invented by your imperfect consciousness?

I have come today to instruct you once again on the Path of knowing the Divine Truth and to draw your attention to what impedes you on the Path of cognizing this Truth.

I AM SHIVA! OM NAMAH SHIVAYA!

You are witnessing the genesis of relations of a new type in each sphere of activities on the planet

April 22, 2009

I AM Shiva! I have come today!

I have come to give a Message, and I have come to assure you that our plans for planet Earth will be fulfilled in spite of the colossal resistance of the opposing forces!

I have come to strengthen our Messenger. I am always there where it is necessary to create a preponderance of forces. I AM Shiva, the destroyer of illusions.

If you want the forces of illusion to leave planet Earth as soon as possible, then you should learn a small Teaching about how you should behave now, in this difficult time.

We are doing our best, and we expect the same from you.

You will notice, and it is impossible not to notice, that the world is changing. And you understand that the process of change will continue, despite the resistance of the opposing forces that are scraping the barrel to use their last resources. The intensity of emotions and the intensity of the conflict require the exertion of all our strength.

And in order for you to maintain yourselves as conductors of the Divine energy, you should get involved in the process of transformation.

There is a popular misconception that the whole process of transformation is inevitable and nothing depends on you. There is a popular opinion that nothing should be undertaken in the physical plane because the physical plane will be destroyed and all life will transit to a more subtle plane.

Yes, it will be so, but allowing it to happen now will mean that ninety percent of humans are not ready for the continuation of their evolution in the subtle plane due to their attachment to the physical plane of planet Earth.

Therefore, no matter how strongly we want to speed up the process of transformation, we cannot do this out of our compassion for Life.

I have come to destroy another illusion in your consciousness. And this is the illusion that you do not need to do anything now.

Do understand that the establishment of harmony between all the bodies is required. And all your bodies must take part in the process of transformation. In order to develop the necessary qualities for the transition to the subtle plane, it is necessary to develop in yourself an ability to perform any task qualitatively and to direct energy for the process of transformation to proceed as smoothly as possible.

You yourselves can regulate the process of changes on the planet. This requires your concentration on the positive, on God, and on the Higher plane of existence. When you think about the Supreme, follow the instructions of the Ascended Masters and work for the Common Good, and then, in this process of joint labor, a new type of relationship will germinate that will replace the old type of relationship that exists on planet Earth now but which must be destroyed.

You are witnessing the genesis of a new type of relationship in every sphere of activity on the planet.

You should understand that God can transform the physical plane of planet Earth only with your help because each of you is a necessary element in the Divine chain. And you will not be able to progress on the path of evolutionary development without establishing a proper order on the physical plane.

Another way of resolving the situation on the planet is a general global cataclysm in which only ten percent of the population of planet Earth will survive and be capable of continuing the evolution in the more subtle planes. In such a case, the rest will join the waste bin of the Universe.

At this moment, each of you decides for yourself which path to follow.

Analyze thoroughly what you are doing during the day and what you are thinking about. Ninety percent of the time you are multiplying the illusion with your thoughts and actions because you are not directing the Divine energy according to the plan of God for planet Earth.

That is why you should more attentively approach everything that surrounds you and everything that you encounter in your lives.

The illusion is now stronger than ever. And you get an impression that it can never be destroyed.

However, if I raise my trident, an end of all the illusory manifestation on the planet will come. I am restraining myself to give every individual a chance.

The barriers that hinder the process of change on the planet are in your consciousness.

Do not hurry to criticize anyone. First look inside yourself, and eventually you will be able to discern. And you will understand that everything that annoys you in the people that surround you is present in yourself because the illusion surrounding you is the illusion inherent in your consciousness. And when you change your consciousness, then your external circumstances start changing.

Now I will reveal a secret to you. You will not die. You will live forever. And the process of the alternation of deaths and births from this moment of time will take place in a different way. You will be born again and remember why you come into embodiment.

We are working on the subtle plane and allow only those souls to be born who agree to act in accordance with the Divine plan. We suspend the embodiment of those souls who resist and do not wish to evolve. By doing this we are creating more favorable conditions on the physical plane, enabling those souls who follow the path of evolution to manifest themselves.

Exactly the same decision was made during the times of Atlantis. And many souls were not allowed to incarnate. Now the cycles have changed, and again favorable conditions for the development of souls must be created on earth.

We are acting very carefully, and we invite you to cooperate.

No matter how long your ego resists, it must be suppressed. And if you yourselves do not manage to master your beast, we will have to put a straightjacket on it for a while, at times, and half of the time.

I AM Shiva!

The Statement of Lord Shiva

May 24, 2009

I AM Shiva!

I have come! I have to make a statement, and I would like you to hear with great attention and respect everything that I wish to convey to you.

First of all, you should make a certain effort to free yourselves from the influence of the illusion surrounding you. You speak with God, so in your minds and hearts only Love and Gratitude to God and the Supreme Law should be present.

You and God. How often can you be face-to-face with God and speak with Him?

I think the experience of our communication today will compel you to take your mind off your illusion and speak with God more often.

Do not think that God will come up to you when you are immersed in the hustle and bustle. Do not think that you will manage to hear the voice of God when you are immersed in your human activities.

There is a considerable difference between the plane in which you reside and the plane in which I reside. And in order for you to approach me, you should steep yourselves in my world. You will be able to understand me only when you manage to raise your vibrations up to the level where I can reside. Therefore, I have come to you now in order to remind you that there is not much time left at your disposal. You must approach with all responsibility the fact that considerable changes are taking place on the planet. And these changes will no

longer allow you to live in the same way that mankind has been living up until now.

Everything that surrounds you in the physical world has not the slightest significance in the spiritual world. And I have come to call you to the spiritual world where there are absolutely different values. Do understand that as long as you are attached to the illusory world you are not able to progress higher. And those of you who are ready in your consciousness for the contact with the Higher worlds, you have nothing to be sorry about and nothing to fear because your souls are ready for the transformation and will enthusiastically accept the changes that are to come. I do not worry about you.

But there are souls who are not ready for the transition, who are lazy about changing their consciousness, and who hesitate to change themselves. They do not even hurry to get rid of such habits as smoking, eating meat, and drinking alcohol. How many of you are dependent on such things?

You will not be able to transit to the New World and to keep your attachments. It is exactly you to whom I have come to appeal this day. You have to understand that there is no time left. The leap into the future world can take place at any moment. Do not throw onto the scale God and Mammon, and do not try to figure out in advance how things will go and how everything will take place. It is not given to you to understand the plan of God with your human consciousness. You must only obey God's Law and bravely follow Him.

Because for you it is the only way out of the corner into which you have painted yourselves. It is to you that I am appealing and it is to you I am giving one more chance.

Stop fussing about, stop running and rushing about. Your state of consciousness will determine your future — your state of consciousness that you will manage to keep in peace, in spite of what is happening now and what will be happening around you.

As to you, my devotees, I would like to ask you to read the mantra "OM NAMAH SHIVAYA." But since there are few true devotees of mine left in the world, the best solution for you is to keep the highest state of consciousness accessible for you. You can find your immortality and the transition to the New World only while keeping the inner devotion to God and the Supreme Law.

Those of you who are grinning while reading my Message and feel doubt and criticism inherent in your carnal mind, I will not be able to bail you out. And your salvation I leave to your own hands.

There are not many people left in the world who can and should be saved. The rest are making their choices themselves or have made their choices already.

The cosmic terms, no matter how long they can seem to be from the human level, still have their beginning and their completion.

Therefore, today as well as a month ago,[5] I have come with the only goal: to give you an opportunity to get

---

[5] The speech is about the dictation of Lord Shiva from April 22, 2009 "You are witnessing the genesis of relations of a new type in each sphere of activities on the planet".

out of the web of the illusory world and to open the door to the Divine world.

The time has come now. Tomorrow may be too late.

I AM Shiva, and I have said everything!

I have come to pull your souls from the darkness that has benighted planet Earth

June 24, 2009

I AM Shiva!

I have come to you again today. It was not worth coming in order to give you the Teaching, because you do not value our Messages and our Teaching.

Every time we encounter the reaction of humanity toward our efforts to establish contact and offer cooperation, we feel like dropping everything and starting from the beginning.

You are not ready and do not want to make the efforts to collaborate.

The illusion still holds control over your beings.

Even when you try to get insight into the subject of our Teaching, you still remain more under the influence of the illusion than under our influence, which we are trying to exert on you through our Messages.

You are not able to overcome the barrier that is invisibly present within you. You do not want and do not wish to take a decisive step and to overcome the illusion in your consciousness. And that is why we are facing a choice: either to leave humanity, to leave it to its own devices, or still continue our efforts and exhortations.

Sometimes it seems to me that it is impossible to rouse humanity by persuasion. However, if we were to give up our control, humanity would not be able to survive on its own even for one Earth-day. You are always under the care of Higher Beings of this Universe.

Your civilization will be destroyed within 24 hours as soon as we stop putting energy into supporting your civilization.

The whole point is that too much effort has already been spent to ensure that humanity starts taking steps in the direction of the evolution and making informed and fairly mature decisions.

Those few souls who are ready to follow our directions are isolated and feel like white crows in the surrounding world. And when I think about these few, when I enjoy the richness of the spiritual experience that they have been gathering like bees over many earthly incarnations, I join the banners of the advocates for the continuation of the earthly experiment.

There is always a little gold, but even though there is much more barren rock, people continue mining gold. And we will continue to allow your aura an opportunity to gain a golden glow.

Amidst the noise, dirt, and dust of your cities, it is very hard to recognize those who are enlightened by the Divine Light. You are looking for God where there is no God and where He cannot be. You are looking for God among the prosperous of the world. However, we come to teach you to be discerning. God is ever present in your world; however, you should observe. Within each of you God is present. You need to observe.

There are very quiet moments of goodness in your life when everything seems to die down. You hear the silence amid the noise of the city. Everything falls into silence. And at such moments God quietly comes to you. He appears from the depths of your being and extends His influence on everything around you. And if you were able to feel such moments of presence of the Divine in your world more often, then having tasted that goodness, you would forever turn away from those surrogates that your civilization offers you. It is impossible to confuse the goodness that God gives you with the surrogates that you meet everywhere in your world.

I wish that you could capture those states of inner silence and tranquility in your world. And I wish that you were able to keep the memory of these states, even when everything around you is collapsing.

There are true states when you abide in God. And you must strive to remain in such states. In this way, the Divine world can pour into your manifested world from inside of you. And then the imperfection of your world will gradually subside like fire that cannot find more fuel for itself.

Only you yourselves make it possible for the imperfection of your world to exist. Only you yourselves direct your energy to the imperfection, and it continues to exist. Stop, wait, and think about what you are doing. Stop running around in circles like a stupid donkey after a carrot from day to day, from embodiment to embodiment. Each of you has his own carrot. For some of you it is sexual pleasures; for others it is your career that you call self-realization for some reason; for others it is narcotic substances, gambling, and entertainment.

Humanity has invented many different things to obstruct the way to the only Truth — God, who dwells in the peace of your hearts.

Enter the peace of your heart. And you will have the standard with which to compare the things you face in your lives. You will compare the states that arise within you when you come across the toys of your world and contrast them with this state of the Divine harmony and quietness.

You need to voluntarily give up all the clutter of different things that are present in your world but are useless for you in the future world.

It is very simple to cut the Gordian knot of your civilization with one blow of the trident. However, every grain of the best human achievements has to be protected and preserved. The best achievements of the human civilization considerably exceed the achievements of other systems of worlds. But as a counterweight in your world, there are so many things that make the Higher Worlds shudder and that should be committed to the cosmic fire.

You are in the crucible of the cosmic furnace. The process of separating gold from waste rock is occurring within you. And the percentage of the golden souls who will transit to the Golden Age of humanity is exactly equal to the percentage of gold in the waste rock on Earth.

I have come in order to pull your souls from the darkness that has benighted planet Earth.

I AM Shiva!

Show your Faith and your Devotion to the Heavens!

December 3, 2009

I AM Shiva!

I AM here and now!

Space and time have obediently given me the opportunity to speak. I have given many Messages through this Messenger. I often worked with the humankind of Earth. I especially love to be in India, my favorite country, where I am worshipped and where I am treated as God.

The inner worship of God is as necessary for you as the breath of life. If you cannot manage to cultivate this feeling of the Divine within yourself, you will not be able to move any further. Your advancement along the path of evolution is inseparably connected with the extent to which you admit the Divinity into your consciousness.

I come to remind you of the simplest truths, without which you will not be able to advance. All the darkness shrouding Earth can be dissolved with one glance of mine. However, you must earn my glance.

Where is your devotion? Where is your diligence? Where is your desire to worship God in everything?

I am speaking about very simple truths. These simple truths must be written on every street corner where billboards display advertisements.

How low society has fallen in just 5000 years of the Kali Yuga!

Within the limits of cosmic history, the degradation of society has reached its zenith in a very short period of time. That is why I come, in order to remind you of the necessity to worship God.

This feeling of the Divine has nothing in common with walking around the temples, mosques, and churches. In order for you to come to your God, you just need to allow this feeling of the Divine into your heart. When you experience this feeling, a sudden silence comes, even if you are in the center of a big city. You experience delight from contemplating God within yourself, and this enables God to reinforce His presence in you. The feeling of Love, the most elevated feeling of Love that you can experience, resembles the Divine feeling.

Now, since I have given you the main direction that you should work on in your lives, I would like to dwell upon another matter of urgency.

And this matter is how could it happen that our presence on the land of our Messenger's Ashram has been blocked? You do not realize what you are doing. Every action directed against our Messenger is perceived as your unwillingness to evolve. You create your karma by every conscious or unconscious action directed against our Messenger. And we have said many times that the karma with our Messenger is equal to the karma with God.

What will you gain by that? The situation on the planet is getting worse. And there is a direct link between the action taken against our Messenger and the worsening of the situation on Earth. How could it happen that our Messenger is on trial? How could it happen that human consciousness was judging the Divine representative?

Oh, woe to those who do not know what they are doing. Oh, woe to all the others who are not aware of the consequences of any actions directed against our Messenger.

I cannot understand your deeds with my own consciousness. You resemble people dancing onboard a ship that is sinking because of a breach. You are trying to find more new toys and amusements, and you take no heed of our words.

I cannot understand it. This is beyond my comprehension. Do you hate the world around you so much that you cause harm to everything indiscriminately? How can you break so far away from the Divine world that you have lost the basic threads of your distinction?

I cannot imagine the situation that humanity is in now. You yourselves have created the whole situation that you are in now with your own hands.

I am telling you that there is another path, an easier and more elevated one. I am telling you what to do in order for this path to open within you. Why do you not hear and understand me?

The allotted time can be prolonged or it can be shortened. We are searching literally bit by bit to collect positive examples that suggest that still there are souls capable of development.

You may not believe me, but sometimes a single example, one feat of a soul in the name of God, is enough to allow an entire civilization to develop. Similarly, one action directed against our representative is enough for the Heavens to turn away and leave humanity to wander in the dark on its own.

The scales are increasingly leaning toward imprudence and unwillingness to follow the Divine Law. Where are the spiritual giants who are incarnated now and who must balance the situation on Earth?

I know many of them who set off skipping toward illusory signs of their greatness, or fell into depression, or considered themselves very great people for whom it is a sin to keep company with the current humanity.

The illusion is very strong, and since the last cycle of Dictations that we gave through our Messenger, it grew even stronger in its position. In this situation a grand manifestation of Faith is needed, the demonstration of your Faith. Show your Faith and your devotion to the Heavens!

You do not need to go to the other end of Earth for this. We see every person who blazes up with the flames of devotion and Service, no matter where they are located on the globe. And we use every person who has prepared his or her temple for Service.

I know many people who are ready. However, they lack bravery and courage in order to rise to their full height and leave the trenches of doing nothing and sitting it out.

I have said enough.

I have come with a cheerless feeling but follow the need to convey the bitter truth to you.

I AM Shiva!

You need to remember that God is most important in your life

January 5, 2010

I AM Shiva!

I have come again! As always, the mercy of Heaven has provided another opportunity for humankind to live up to its promise.

We all are paying close attention to what is happening on the planet now. The secret is in the fact that Earth has received a new portion of the Divine energy. We are paying close attention to the effect that it will have on humankind of planet Earth. Will humankind continue its path to nowhere, or will it come to reason and finally follow the advice of the Great Masters of humanity to which I also have the honor of belonging?

It is not often that I have the opportunity to give my Messages. That is why I always strive to include in my Messages the greatest possible impulse of energy that could prompt you to awaken and move forward along the ascending spiral of evolution.

You have noticed that this new cycle of Messages we are giving through our Messenger does not give a lot of food for the mind, the carnal mind. We have begun to act in a more subtle way in order to awaken those individuals who are capable of responding to new energies, more subtle energies.

The first layer of our Messages has awakened a certain number of individuals. Now new energies aimed at another level of people have started to come through.

We need the very best people who are incarnated now. In your past incarnations you had the experience of Service, and many of you served the Hierarchy for more than one incarnation. The surrounding physical world has changed, but you must remember your mission and, after receiving the impulse of these Messages into your hearts, overcome the outer circumstances and remove everything from yourselves that hinders your Service.

It is difficult for you, and many of you have already burdened yourselves with a karmic load that you will have to carry with you until the end of your current incarnation. However, there are those who have not burdened themselves in any way but are trying to find food for their souls in the surrounding illusion. These people either go from one teaching to another or change jobs, trying to find some satisfaction in external-world activities.

All this is vain. You have already gained experience of worldly work in many past incarnations. You need to remember that the most important thing in your life is God. And you need to devote all your life only to the fulfillment of God's plans.

It cannot be that you serve God and simultaneously leave some external activity for yourselves in the world, trying to gain some more experience and obtain another toy. It is a big step back for you. Do not look at the people who surround you. Compared to you, they are still in kindergarten while you have already graduated from the university. You need to understand that the most important and determining characteristic for you is your level of consciousness and not the external attributes of acknowledgement or prosperity that are currently common in your world. There are eternal values, and there are temporary illusionary pursuits.

You remind me of grown-up men and women sitting in a sandbox and trying to build sand castles and make sand sculptures.

Wake up. There are real things that you should be doing, things that correspond to your level of consciousness.

The more you try to postpone making your final decision and the more you try to hide behind different forms of activity in the illusionary world, the more painful and difficult the sobering process will be for you when one day, maybe even this year, you wake up and feel the breath of eternity.

You need to devote your entire life to Service.

Those who cannot do it have not reached your level of consciousness.

Everyone is at his or her own level of consciousness development, but if you do not take the level that is appropriate for you, then the rest will not have a model in the physical plane that they will be able to follow.

Billions of people live on planet Earth. Yet, only very few of them are brave enough to climb to the top of Chomolungma, the highest peak in the world. The rest prefer to watch entertainment shows on TV that replace real life for them.

There is always room for heroic acts in your lives. You perform a heroic act every day when you perform God's work on Earth, despite any external circumstances, despite feeling unwell, and despite any illnesses.

In order to perform God's work, you do not need to climb to the top of Chomolungma. You need to take on the first project — a very simple project — that is lying right in front of your nose and begin implementing it. It may seem to you that this work is not worth doing, that it is too small and inconspicuous.

Try to understand that when you perform small deeds with great love, you open an opportunity of greater Service for yourselves.

Masters cannot trust you with the work for the Brotherhood before they thoroughly test you, and that takes more than one or two years. And even if you have already been trusted by the Brotherhood in your past incarnations and performed their tasks, in this incarnation you will have to earn the trust again and prove that you are worthy of this trust.

Many of you are searching for an activity that you can do. Many are searching for people with whom you can do something. Believe me; you do not need any of that. You already have everything you need to begin your Service. God has taken care of everything already. All you need to do is to open your eyes and see the work that you need to start doing.

We are casting out our nets again and waiting to see what kind of catch we will have this time.

I AM Shiva!

It is not the work with the Ascended Hosts that allows you to move along the Path, it is the quality of your consciousness

December 25, 2010

I AM Shiva!

I have come!

You think that our work of transmitting Messages to your world is trivial. You think that everyone can hear from the finer world if they want to.

You are right. But all that becomes possible only under certain conditions and in making certain commitments.

Everything is very simple: You have to dedicate your whole life to Serving the Masters not only in your words but also in practice. Your whole life.

Are you ready to obey all of our requirements?

Yes, many of you will agree and say that you are ready.

To start with, keep your consciousness at the highest possible level every day. Try this simple practice. And when you decide to do it, at the end of the day, take a seat quietly and ask yourself. "How many times have you condemned your neighbor for the day? How many times have you been irritated? How many times have you been dissatisfied with your boss, your neighbors, or the government of your country?"

If that task seems very easy for you to do and in your sly way you state that you have fulfilled all the given conditions, then answer my simple questions: "Are you satisfied with your life? Are you grateful to God for everything that happens in your life?"

Think about what I am getting at. I am trying to bring to your modern consciousness the ancient Truth that one of your first steps and achievements on the Path will be your unfailing feeling of satisfaction with everything around you and within you.

For many of you the question arises whether it is possible to fulfill the given task under the conditions of modern society.

How is it possible to feel satisfaction if the prevailing feeling in society is the opposite: dissatisfaction with life, society, the government, the president, the boss at work … everything?

Long ago in ancient times your souls chose to rebel against the Divine Law. You tore yourselves away from the Divine reality and went toward satisfaction of your ego's whims. That was long ago.

But God is very merciful and patient. And you were given an opportunity to manifest humility toward the Divine Law and to get back on the Path of Truth for many of your incarnations.

But every time, your souls — the souls of those people who are incarnated now — refused the given opportunity and preferred to use every life for satisfying their escalating desires.

With every incarnation you stood in front of more and more severe external conditions.

So why are you surprised? You created the conditions that you are in nowadays with your choices in many of your incarnations. And now, for many of you, it seems an impracticable requirement to show even elementary achievements on the way of apprenticeship.

We have been waiting long enough. We have hoped that humanity would be able to use the given knowledge in order to start along the Path we showed.

What do we observe? We see a mass of people who try to get Messages, pretend to be a guru, and gather people in order to communicate truth.

The Divine Grace of giving the Messages to your world is too expensive for the Ascended Hosts to keep more than one or two Messengers simultaneously. At your time, when people cannot distinguish elementary things, giving Messages is a very big risk.

Of course, we run the risk of subjecting the Messenger as a person to numerous accusations, but to a greater extent we put at risk the people who oppose our Messenger. For them, karma is so heavy that it can hardly be worked off in the foreseeable future.

We told you about the conditions for sending Messages to your world, and we told you about the quality of recompense that you need to earn in order to rise to the next evolutionary stage.

Believe me, you and the Ascended Hosts have different weight categories. No matter what steps your ego takes to avoid the Divine Law and the order existing in this Universe, it will not succeed.

The only way that is commanded for your time is to perfect yourself in God. And initiations have never been passed by masses of people. The Path of Initiations is an individual path. And together or in a team you can only go right in the opposite direction, as they say, to hell.

So, summarizing our talk today, I would like to draw your attention to the fact that there are certain milestones, stages of the Path that allow an individual to be trusted by the Ascended Hosts in order to Serve.

You may think that you have already passed all necessary initiations and have been working under the direction of the Ascended Masters for a long time. The illusion of your time may lead you to believe that you are a messenger or work under the direction of the Ascended Masters. Therefore, your task in the near future is to take a detached view of yourself and understand exactly where you are on the Path. And perhaps it is time for you to start playing with some less dangerous toys.

It is not the work with the Ascended Hosts that allows you to move along the Path; it is the quality of your consciousness. Believe me; your world gives you an opportunity in your everyday life to gain all of the necessary qualities that allow one to pass the necessary initiations at the School of Mysteries in the pyramid.

Today our talk touched upon the problems that are very real for many people. For others, this talk may allow them to have a wider outlook and better clarity of judgement.

I AM Shiva!

The only thing that can save humankind now is your confidence in the existence of the Higher Reality

June 21, 2011

I AM Shiva!

I have come!

Shiva I AM.

Today we will talk about the most important thing! We will talk about that which is eternal and everlasting. And this aspect of the Divine reality must engross your mind.

It is because all the other aspects of your life are subject to change — and they will be changed. Each of you sooner or later will be confronted with the questions: Where do you aspire to be? Which world do you prefer?

You stay in a vanishing illusory world only as long as you wish to stay in it. And many individuals who live on Earth do not even think about the fact that another reality exists, a world that is imperceptible to physical senses.

However, it is exactly this reality that is the primary and determining reality, no matter how difficult it is for you to believe in the true Divine reality. Therefore, the most important question that you have to solve for yourself now is the question of which reality you want to give preference to. Many will think that the time to answer this question has not yet come and that they still have enough time to enjoy a sweet sleep in the illusion.

No, beloved. It is now that the time has come when you must decide in your consciousness and make a choice. And from this seemingly abstract choice, the entire course of the further evolution on planet Earth depends.

Imagine that you work in a company. And your firm has certain plans and goals. If you are hired by this firm, you have to share those plans and goals. Then you will be able to participate in the activities of the company and contribute to the implementation of the common goals and tasks. If you suddenly start being guided by other goals that are not in accordance with the common goals of the company, then you risk being fired.

The same analogy exists in your situation in the world now. I and the other Beings of Light come to you and remind you repeatedly that you live in a universe that exists according to the laws that are characteristic of this Universe. And the main Laws of this Universe are Serving your neighbors, Compassion, and Mercy on the basis of unconditional Love and unselfishness.

This is a given; those conditions were predetermined when this Universe began the cycle of its existence.

You, as beings endowed with free will, decided to make your own adjustments to the general plan for the development of this Universe. You over-focused on your ego and on satisfying its desires and whims. And the more pleasure you gave yourselves, the more and more you were losing touch with the general Divine plan for this Universe. Over time, you plunged so deeply into the illusion created by your own mind that you do not even believe that there can be another reality that is based on the Law of Love and unselfishness.

You think that the problems of your society are to do with terrorism, crimes, drugs, corruption or whatever else that is typical of your society and provokes disputes and arguments.

No, beloved, there is only one problem that you are currently facing and that requires an immediate solution. This is the problem of your detachment from the Higher world and unwillingness to overcome the things that prevent you and the whole human society from returning to the path of evolutionary development predetermined by the Creator of this Universe.

It seems to you that I am talking about abstract things because you cannot believe in what you cannot feel and see with your eyes. But I am telling you that the situation that your society is now in can be saved by your Faith in what is invisible. And these are the only things that can save humanity now: your confidence in the existence of the Higher reality and your aspiration to this reality. Then, when you believe and aspire, you will be able to solve all the problems of your society from the position of the Higher reality. When this approach is applied in all spheres of human activity, then positive changes will begin in society.

You should start with yourself, from your personal relationship with God who is within you. Then, when you establish your personal relationship with the inner God, your life will begin to change. It is your choice that you must make immediately. It is impossible to force you to make your choice. We can only warn you about the fact that, sooner or later, the existing Law will make you return to the real world by changing the conditions of your world.

This is a very simple truth. This truth is so simple that none of the political forces or organizations that exist in your world considers this truth seriously. The very thing that can change the situation on the planet in the shortest amount of time is not considered by people seriously. More than that, sometimes this simple truth causes fear and aggression. The blame for this lies in that sad fact that humankind is wrapped up in ignorance, despite all the modern inventions of your mechanistic civilization.

I am telling you that there is no longer a possibility for the mechanistic civilization to exist on the planet. The resources of the planet and the state of its subtle bodies can no longer withstand your experiments. And, having lost the physical platform for existence, humankind will put the clock of its evolution back for many millions of years.

This is the key reason why the Beings of Light come to you and give their directions. We do this out of Compassion for you and your souls.

Now I say goodbye to you.

I AM Shiva!

Now your work for God is starting

June 22, 2012

I AM Shiva!

I have come!

Today I wish that you will listen to me not because I want it so much but because the time has come when I must tell you this.

So, every time during my coming, exactly as during the coming of every Master, a miracle of communication between our worlds takes place. Each time there is a release of Light in the place where our Messages are received. The blessings that illuminate Earth at this moment of transmission of my Message will not fail to influence the destinies of peoples of Earth.

I have come today at that time when our Messenger is staying in the land of Latvia. And I have come at the moment when the sun itself is favorable to the maximal transmission of my energies to this land.

With every receiving and reading of a Message, you have an opportunity to receive a blessing. And this is something that cannot be expressed in words. It is something that is imparted without words from my heart to your hearts.

Be blessed. Accept the gift of my heart.

You are to accomplish a great deal. It is exactly now that the time has come when the whole further course of evolution on planet Earth depends on each of you who are in embodiment. A crucial turn of energies takes place in your octave. What was descending should now start its upward ascension to our world, to the world of the Ascended Hosts.

It is with your hands and your feet that this great turn of the cosmic cycle must take place in the near future. As the Lord responsible for the contraction of the illusion, I am ready to impart the knowledge of ancient times to you.

Each of you becomes irreplaceable, each of you who is able and ready to accept my words and my energies. For the time has come. At this moment all the Ascended Hosts are observing the evolution on planet Earth. The most critical moment in the history of the planet has come. And the choice of each of you at this moment determines the future of the whole planet.

It is that choice that you must make now.

I am telling you that there is nothing more important in your life that you could do. Give up all the fuss that is around you.

Focus your consciousness on the highest possible point that you can reach. Think about the eternal.

Think about immense and infinite God.

Think about His Greatness.

You are a part of God.

He can reside in each of you.

With your help, the Creator of this Universe will be able to turn the cosmic cycles.

Think about the greatness of the forthcoming mission. Each of you can and is able to fulfill the grandiose plan of God concerning the contraction of the illusion.

The time has come and the cycles have turned. The time has come for the contraction of the illusory world. Just like the time when Creation began, the turning point has come when Creation is to be contracted. Space and time are starting a new cycle. The illusion is beginning its contraction.

Each of you is called upon to take part in this process of contraction of the illusion. It is impossible for me or for any of the Ascended Masters to reside in your world now. The world is too rough and its vibrations are too low. Only you can do this work for the world. Only you, by your choices and your actions, are able to start this work on the contraction of the illusion.

Only with the help of your consciousness can God do this work, a grandiose work requiring millions of years for its accomplishment.

You are given the opportunity to proceed to this mission now. If you read all of the Dictations that we have given through our Messenger during these years, you will find all the necessary recommendations in them in order for you to accomplish your work and to fulfill your Divine purpose.

Each Dictation contains the knowledge and information that you need now. There is hidden knowledge that lies between the lines which is unpacked in your consciousness when you are asleep or awake over many years.

The key that I will give you today is lying on the surface. The daily choices that you make, every choice you make and all your actions during the day, if they have a Divine character, produce exactly the work that you are called to fulfill. If you still prefer to focus on the illusion, on pleasures and entertainment, or on the whims of your ego no matter how they are expressed, then you stand in opposition to God and His plans.

Every thought of yours is important.

Every feeling of yours is important.

Every action that you take is important.

Now your work for God is starting. Any action or attention directed toward the illusory world will stand in opposition to the plans of God.

Any action directed to Common Weal and Good will be welcomed by Heaven and will serve as a sign for us that humankind is capable of evolutionary development and the new stage of its development.

Now a great deal depends on your awareness, your aspirations, and your faith. I have come to you today in order to remind you of your duty and your work that nobody but you can do — the grandiose work on the contraction of the illusion. And this is your most important job: to separate what is eternal from what is transient in your consciousness.

Your work to separate the reality from the illusion inside of you and outside of you is of major importance now. Your energy flows where your attention is directed. If you are constantly focused on the illusory world, then you are working against God and multiplying the illusion.

If you are constantly focused of the Supreme, Divine world, then all Heavens will glorify you.

The time has come when the Heavens look forward to your work.

Please, realize your responsibility and start right now. You have all the knowledge. Get started!

Every moment you are creating. You are managing your energy. You only need to attune to God in order for your flow of energy to always be in the Divine flow.

I AM Shiva!

I have come to give you a Teaching about God

December 22, 2012

I AM Shiva!!!

I have come!

I have come as always in might and in all my fullness!

I AM Shiva!

Today I must tell you about the Truth, which your consciousness is not able to take in so far. But if you meditate long enough and persistently on this Truth, then gradually you will become the manifestation of this Truth yourself.

I have come to give you a Teaching about God because in this world and in all other worlds there is nothing but God. The state of consciousness that you possess now is the only thing that separates you from God and the Divine Truth.

If you meditate on God and the Divine Truth every day, then you will be able to express this Truth in your world more fully and completely.

The task of your embodiment is to enable the Divine Truth to manifest through you, through your entire being!

How to do it? How can you fulfill the task of your embodiment?

Of course, my words seem strange and meaningless for many of you. However, if this is the case, then your consciousness is just thoroughly blocked from the Divine Truth. And you should immediately start taking measures in order to restore your right state of consciousness and the right guidelines in your life.

Imagine a person who is lost in the forest. The usual world is left far behind. There is a totally different reality around him: a thick jungle, impassable bushes, and tall trees. Neither sun nor horizon is visible. It is dusk that reigns, and the smell of dampness and mustiness is in the air; not a breath of wind, not a ray of light.

Your state of consciousness resembles the state of consciousness of a person who is lost in the woods. In the same way, you are deep in the thickets of the illusion and do not know in which direction to move. It seems to you that you have come across a path that will hopefully lead you out of the thickets. It is similar to how you grasp at the first-found teaching or faith. You hear familiar words about God, and they evoke a response in the innermost depths of your being. Yet, in a while you understand that you are mistaken. The path has turned out to be another illusion of your consciousness.

Once again you fall into despair. You beg God to reveal the Path to you. It seems to you that everything is already hopeless. There is no strength to overcome the fear, the dusk of your human consciousness, and the jungle all around you. The illusion completely takes hold of your consciousness. It seems to you that nothing can change your way of living. Everything seems dull and ordinary: wild howls of the city jungle, grinding sounds of the brakes, fears and rustles.

You soul cries out, "How long, Lord, can one keep bearing it?"

Then, when it seems that nothing in the whole world is pleasant, when all the surroundings seem hostile and unfriendly, the Path must be revealed and the Divine Truth must come in sight. Not somewhere outside of you and your being. The Truth is revealed within. Indeed, it really looks like a flash of a supernova.

It is the transition to a new level of consciousness.

It is illumination!

It is joy!

It is happiness!

It is bliss!

How many of you have already experienced this state?

How many of you are looking forward to this state?

I know, and you must become aware, that the first flashes of illumination will be followed by years of testing. You will be trying to regain the state of bliss that you have experienced. You will strive to acquire it again. It may be that until the end of your current embodiment you will not be able to return to this state of freedom from the sleep in the illusion.

However, I must tell you that it is not this state of ecstasy and bliss that you should aspire to. You must find within yourselves a more stable state of inner self-confidence, dignity, nobleness, harmony, and tranquility.

This is truly the state that will help you cope with any difficulties and trials. You must strive to acquire a point of balance, a foothold within yourselves. This is vital because if you do it, if you find a foothold within yourselves, then you will always be calm even when the whole world is stormy.

This foothold is the connection with your authentic essence, with your Divine essence, with God within you.

When you acquire this state of balance and peace, you will win a great victory! You can lose this state for a little while, you can be immersed in the illusion again and again, yet you will already know where you should aspire.

It is similar to a compass that will guide you when you get lost in the woods. If you keep moving in one direction, then sooner or later you will scramble out of the jungle, and your wanderings in the dusk of the illusion will cease.

Pay heed to the fact that you must constantly make efforts to advance toward reality. You cannot aspire to and go along the Path on one day and then have a day off on the next day.

If you do not constantly make efforts to come out of the forest where you got lost, then you risk not coming out of the woods at all. Predatory animals are looking forward to the moment when you relax and fall asleep.

Similarly, if you stop making daily efforts in the world that you live in, and predatory animals of your insatiable desires start approaching you, then it will be good if you suddenly remember that you need to continue moving.

All landmarks on your Path are known.

All dangers are identified.

You should just find the power within yourselves and begin moving.

Do understand that not everything is ideal in your world. To be precise, everything is very far from perfection. Therefore, the first and foremost thing will be your aspiration to acquire the gift of distinction, the Divine vision.

If you carefully choose and select everything that surrounds you in your world, if you care about the quality and the vibrations of the things that surround you, of the food that you consume, of the people with whom you communicate, of the books that you read, of the music that you listen to, then over time the space that you have created around you will start helping and supporting you at those moments when you lose your inner guidelines.

Everything in your life has a meaning.

Everything should be treated very carefully.

Sometimes one object that you fix your eyes on at a difficult moment is enough to change your vibrations, and then you enter the field of higher, Divine vibrations.

Now the time has come when much depends on each of your choices, on each of your steps, and on each of your thoughts.

The circumstances on the planet have changed.

It is necessary to be very cautious.

I AM Shiva!

The time for your actions has come!

June 21, 2014

I AM Shiva!

Today, on this day of the summer solstice, I have come to you!

As always, I am adamant and full of determination.

My requirements for those who follow us are increasing every day.

This is quite obvious. Only a few years ago we tried to teach and guide you, but now the time of your training is over; the time has come for decisive actions.

There is no opportunity to complete your education any longer.

I am telling you that the situation has become tense every day and even every hour.

Right now the moment has come for which many of you have come into embodiment.

The balance of the planet is on the verge of collapse.

Peace on Earth is literally hanging by a hair.

Instead of firmly standing up for the Divine world and against the world of illusion, many of our followers decided to have a rest, as though nothing is happening in the world.

I am telling you that the opposing forces are doing everything so that further evolutionary development on planet Earth becomes impossible.

I am telling you that exactly now the time has come when you must apply all your efforts, all your abilities, talents, and skills to restore the inner balance of powers and to get to the all-out attack in the external world.

You must return the Divine order into your world!

If you still pretend that nothing is happening, if you ignore your duty of sustaining the Divine patterns on the planet, then you will lose your planet — the platform on which the development of billions of souls is taking place.

You are responsible for planet Earth!

You must stop doing nothing!

We have run out of the time planned for peaceful Teaching!

The time has come for decisive actions!

Show what you have learned in the 10 years that you have been trained under the guidance of the Ascended Hosts!

The balance on the planet could be maintained with the help of Prayer Vigils. I personally asked you through our Messenger to give this energy to the Masters during the Prayer Vigil on March 23rd of this year.

If only ten thousand people had supported my appeal, we could have turned the situation on the planet back to a peaceful course, even during the days of the spring equinox.

However, we could not find even two thousand people praying.

First, any negative manifestation forming in the subtle plane can be neutralized with the help of prayers. But then comes the moment when negative energies start to precipitate on the physical plane. At this moment, not only prayer work is needed from you but also your work in the physical plane.

The repulsion of negative energies must be created in every plane of existence!

I will remind you of the Law. When the Great Masters of humanity come to give the Teaching to incarnated humankind, they always do this before global negative processes are about to happen on Earth.

We always give humankind a chance to go along the easiest path by changing its own consciousness.

We give the Teaching that makes it possible to change the consciousness of a sufficient number of incarnated individuals in a few years.

We spend a great deal of Divine energy transmitting our Messages into your world.

However, the moment comes when humanity refuses to go along the royal road.

More and more individuals that we had hoped for are tempted by the magic of the illusion and leave the Path.

The moment has come.

When humanity makes a collective choice not to advance in an easier direction by changing their consciousness, then the Law of Karma comes into effect.

Any karma can be softened at the level of thought and emotions. To do this, you should acknowledge mistakes and show repentance.

When the easier path is rejected, the release of karma begins on the physical plane. And periodically, it happens in a more intense way than it usually does.

Every time before another world war, we obtain the consent of the Supreme Council of this Universe and get a dispensation for the transmission of our Teaching. We do this hoping that humanity will agree to follow the path of changing their consciousness.

However, our attempts fail every time, and we cannot reach and persuade the necessary number of incarnated individuals to follow the Path shown by us.

The realization of karma always follows the rejection.

I must tell you that it is possible to get back to the easier path at any moment. I must also tell you that wars, catastrophes, and natural disasters are not God's punishment.

All these incidents are born of the consciousness of the people who are incarnated now. So the retribution, as the consequence, unavoidably follows the cause that has created it.

The change in people's consciousness will occur in any case. It is as inevitable as the sunrise. However, the question is this: How much suffering is required for humanity to learn their lessons?

I give you this Message hoping that at least a small number of our disciples will manage to unite and start acting.

You have to stop any manifestation of the opposing forces in all planes of being and in all spheres of human activity.

The more you act in unity, the more avoidable the deaths, violence, and misery will be.

The time for your actions has come! Now!

I AM Shiva!

Every day ask God to be with you and to guide your whole life

December 21, 2014

I AM Shiva!!!

I have come!

Today! On this day!

I am glad that, thanks to the Divine mercy, I can come again to give my directions, which I am sure will help you at this difficult time for humankind of Earth.

So, I have come.

Now, when you are better adapted to my energies, I have to talk about the main reason of my visit today.

All of you who have read our Messages for all these years are already familiar with the main Teaching that we are giving. It refers to the Teaching on the choice and the Path.

Many souls are incarnated now on planet Earth.

For every soul there comes a time when it must make a choice. And this choice will determine its future destiny, the energy level at which this soul will either continue its evolution or will cease it.

Divine mercy is boundless. At the moment, there are a great number of souls in embodiment, and for many of them this is the last opportunity to continue their evolutionary development.

Of course, almost all of the souls have already decided on their choice. And of course, it is very difficult sometimes, being in the hustle and bustle, to understand the entire reality and seriousness of the choice made.

You can understand that sometimes it is unbearably hard to watch how many people are literally killing themselves and destroying their souls. The energies that are in their auras and are determined by the succession of their choices in past incarnations literally force these individuals to make low-grade choices.

It is exactly for this, in order to help even a small number of individuals change their destiny that we continue to come and give our Teaching.

It is very difficult to understand many simple Truths that we are giving because many Truths are easy to understand only at a certain energy level. To reach this level you need a certain degree of solitude, and you must not be under the influence of mass consciousness. Very few people have such a luxury as solitude, and very few are not under the influence of the negativity that is prevailing in the world.

I will tell you more. As soon as people break out of the vanity of their everyday lives and get a chance to spend at least several days in solitude and prayer, the very state of getting closer to the Divine arouses fear and discomfort within them

It would appear that you approached God, your vibrations rose, your consciousness elevated, but discomfort, depression, and fear started to encircle you densely.

Why is it so, beloved?

You are living in this negative environment because your karmic energies attract you to this environment. When, thanks to the Divine mercy, you get into more harmonious conditions, your karmic energies rise and deprive you of an opportunity to enjoy your contact with God living within you!

Facing unexplainable states of their consciousness at the moment that seems very close to the Divine world, many spiritual seekers stop their spiritual practices in fear and return to their habitual environment, typical in the mass consciousness.

Beloved, I have come to tell you that at this time an abyss of reasonableness is now separating you from the Divine world.

It is very hard for you to understand me because you are in an upside-down world, an imperfect world — literally in a cesspool.

Yet, I am asking you simply to believe me and to continue moving — on your Faith and Love.

It is always hard to move in total darkness and unfavorable weather conditions. However, if you start moving in the chosen direction and continue to go surmounting yourself, then later on you will see the sunrise and everything will start changing and reviving around you.

Believe me, at the very beginning it is very hard to break out of the fog of the veil of illusion surrounding you. When the rays of the dawn of the Divine consciousness start illuminating the twilight of your being with the light of reason, you acquire distinction of the Light from the darkness, the reality from the illusion.

All of you lack faith and aspiration. These fundamental and necessary qualities on the Path are the main targets of the forces opposite to us and are attacked through the media, television, and the Internet.

You are palmed off to surrogates, and you cannot distinguish between Divine Light and lights of advertising, between true values and the tinsel of a mass holiday.

Only few of you are able to oppose the forces of illusion with your devotion and aspiration.

It is impossible to develop the qualities that lead your soul to liberation from the shackles of illusion within one incarnation. However, if you do not start cultivating these qualities within yourself, you risk never getting out of the trap of illusion.

Imagine that you are in a mystery school. All the inhabitants of planet Earth are in a gigantic school for initiates.

You, each of you, can count on your own efforts only. You face dangers every day. Every day you make your choice, the only choice between the world of God and the world of illusion. There are millions of choices, but the essence of them is reduced to the only choice: whether you choose eternity or you choose decay.

So, the purpose of my visit today was to direct your being toward the real world.

You must devote every day of your life only to God, to God that resides within you, and to God that resides within every living being.

Only one thought must be in your mind when you wake up: "I am with God!"

Only this thought can shield you from the forces of illusion throughout your day.

Only permanent concentration on God can tear you out of the nets of illusion.

Tirelessly, every day ask God to be with you and to guide your whole life and all your choices.

Only God can help you and your soul at this difficult time in the twilight of human consciousness.

I AM Shiva!

Only faith in God and love for all of Creation can save humanity in the near future

December 21, 2015

I AM Shiva!

Today I have come!

Most regrettably, I have come in order to share sad news with you.

Well! All in this world is only an illusion.

You yourselves choose the illusion that you reside in.

Your illusion is formed with your consciousness. If you wish to constantly reside in fear, hatred, and anger, then the illusion that surrounds you adjusts to your consciousness, and you receive the reflection of your imperfection in the outer world in the form of wars, terrorism, social tension, and financial instability.

You choose all that for yourselves, beloved.

It is your choice.

Our task is only to invite you to Our table and to offer Our viands.

However, you can refuse and not accept them.

This is the Law of free will.

Over the past 10 years the dispensation was active that allowed Us not only to come and give Our instruction in the form of Messages but also to transmit Our energies into your world.

You were only required to agree to instruction and follow our recommendations.

<...>

When you refuse the Divine models, the opposite tendencies in the world increase immediately.

You refuse morality and receive completely immoral manifestations of your world: the lying politicians and economists, the increase of terrorism, and the unfolding of wars.

Let me remind you that you live in the world of consequences. Each of your choices leads to corresponding results.

The missed opportunities turn into a humanitarian disaster that you have been facilitating by any means.

In this way, the leaders of humanity who have been reading our Messages all this time have made their choice.

We lost.

Of course, you will have to face the consequences of your choice.

When you do not fulfill the plan of the Masters, when you do not follow the voice of your conscience, when you choose doubts and laziness, then you receive consequences, and these consequences will increase more and more starting next year.

I would like to clarify for you one more aspect of our Teaching that concerns the karma with our Messenger.

When Our Messenger gets persecuted, discredited, or accused, it creates a tremendous karma, equivalent to the level of karma with God.

As it is known, God deprives intelligence to those whom He wishes to punish.

Insanity can take over not only a single person but also entire countries and nations.

You observed that many times throughout the history of humankind. Fascism and communism are such diseases of insanity of peoples and nations.

The karma of godlessness and the karma of accusations toward our Messenger is one of the most severe kinds of karma.

I have come today in order to explain to your consciousness the cause of the events that are coming, and each of you who read our Messages took part in the creation of these events.

The insanity of countries generates wars and their consequences — famine and humanitarian disasters.

Can this be avoided?

It can. For that, you need to accept the supremacy of the Divine Law in your lives.

There is only one Truth. All genuine prophets, Messengers, and missions throughout the entire history of the development of humankind carried only one Divine Truth: about God who is everything that surrounds you.

It is about God inside of you and God outside of you.

Only faith in God and love for all of Creation can save humanity in the near future.

Now I must leave you.

The burden of karma must come down on humankind in the form of the cover of darkness.

The suffering can purify the consciousness in the same way as prayer and repentance.

I AM Shiva!

A Teaching on the focus of Light

June 20, 2016

I AM Shiva!

I have come on this day of the summer solstice!

For you, I am ready to overcome all difficulties and obstacles so that you can enjoy our contact.

Now, I wish that you would concentrate all of your strength and abilities of your soul.

Get away from your fussy thoughts.

Put out the flames of desires.

Keep contradictory feelings away.

Enjoy the inner peace.

Eternity.

The breath of Eternity.

Breathe in…

Breathe out…

Connect to the breath of the Universe.

Right now, I want to share the Teaching of the Masters with you.

The subject of our talk today will be something that you cannot touch, and many of you are not even able to feel it.

You have to take that on trust.

And if you do not want to believe, then there is no point in you reading and listening to my Message.

So, in our Messages, especially at the beginning of the work of our Messenger, We have mentioned the concept of the focus of Light.

You remember that the focus of Light was moved from America to Russia in 2005.

What is this focus of Light?

I will give you the Teaching on this subject today.

The focus of Light is the ability to transmit the Divine energy. This is a real point in space and time that allows a huge amount of the Divine energy to pass into the physical world.

The amount of the Divine energy is quite enough to make any changes in any country of the world.

However, certain requirements must be met for the implementation of these changes.

To begin with, the focus of Light is not anchored somewhere in the physical world. It is not a rock and not a building.

143

The focus of Light is anchored in the bodies of our Messenger.

This is her ability to transmit Light into the physical world, and it is an ability that was deserved in many previous incarnations and also in this lifetime.

The ability to transmit Light does not mean that the Light, the Divine energy, will enter the dense world.

No, the decision of the Supreme Council of the Universe and the decision of the Karmic Board are necessary in order to provide the Divine energy.

At the moment the focus of Light, anchored in the subtle bodies of our Messenger, passes not more than 10 percent of its designed capacity.

Why?

This is because there are no conditions in the physical plane for the implementation of Our plans.

We told you about the opportunity that had been given to Russia in 2005.

However, in order to realize the opportunity, the conditions in the physical plane must be created.

Several times we asked you to take care of our Messenger.

Devoted hearts are needed for this; the hearts that are ready to sacrifice much for the sake of the mission of Light and the plans of the Masters.

How does the focus of Light work?

First, aspiring and devoted hearts must be found.

Then, on the feelings of Love, gratitude, respect, and honor toward our Messenger, they can get a part of the Divine energy that our focus of Light is spreading in the physical world.

With the growth in the number of people who can perceive our energies, we increase the power of the source of the energy, and we start pumping the energy through the focus of Light into the physical world.

Each devoted disciple of ours receives more and more of the Divine energy. This is similar to how a nuclear power plant flows current through wires to enable the operation of many objects and units, mechanisms, and machinery, and it gives light to buildings and streets.

In the same way, Divine energy fills the space through the hearts of those who are ready. The vibrations of the physical plane change, and many things that happen on Earth now will be impossible when the space becomes full of Divine Light.

This is similar to the fact that it is more difficult for criminals to manage their dark business in the light of day.

However, what We expected did not happen.

Our Teaching was not in demand among people.

Although many people read our Messages, there are no people among them who bear the flame of Service in its fullness within their hearts.

I will say it again: The flame of Service can only flare up based on the qualities of absolute devotion to the Masters, to our Messenger, and on the qualities of love, gratitude, and honor.

For the last 10 years, we have not managed to gather a sufficient number of hearts devoted to us.

Therefore, the focus of Light could not work at its full capacity.

That is why people did not get enough energy to transform the physical plane.

After that attempt of violence against our Messenger in 2012, I ordered her to leave Russia immediately.

Therefore, the Divine opportunity is now withdrawn from the territory of Russia.

The focus of Light has been moved from Russia.

Human intelligence tends to associate the prosperity of a country, or an economic miracle that takes place in a particular country, with achievements in science, technology, management, or the discovery of advanced technologies.

However, these are only the consequences of the fact that the people in that country allow the Messengers of the Masters to stay on their territory.

Not all of our Messengers are shown. Many of them are completely unknown. However, they could work and transmit Divine energy where it was necessary according to the plans of the Masters.

But when our Messengers are pursued, persecuted, and are not honored, then the country stands in front of an abyss.

It is possible to change the situation at any moment.

God has unlimited reserves of energy needed for transformation.

However, all transformations in the physical plane can only be realized through the hearts of people, through their hands and feet.

That is why it is said that the future depends on everyone — literally on every person who is reading these lines.

Since Russia is the key country on which the changes for the future of the entire planet depend, the lack of changes in Russia will manifest on the entire planet in the near future.

This time the Divine opportunity has not been realized.

Will there be another one? And when?

This depends on each of you, beloved.

I AM Shiva!

The reaping time

June 21, 2016

I AM Shiva!

I have come again!

In order for our communication to take place, please get yourself into the proper state of consciousness.

I am fully aware that few in your time are able to raise their consciousness to the level where it would be possible to perceive the energies of the Ascended Masters.

Yes, beloved, your world has separated itself from the Divine world to such an extent that every time it becomes harder and harder for Us to find those hearts who are able to perceive Our energies and therefore, to grasp the meaning of the Teaching being given by Us.

Unfortunately, the thing that is happening in the world today can be compared to totally worshipping the golden calf.

Everything surrounding you, especially in large cities, is only the scenery where you are presented with this single dominant world religion — namely, the religion of worshipping the golden calf.

We have talked many times in dozens of Messages about the fact that the illusion surrounding you obediently adjusts to your consciousness. However, your consciousness is formed by the illusion surrounding you.

Therefore, if you are constantly staying in a large city, you cannot be free from the vibrations surrounding you. You obediently follow the way of life and the stereotypes that surround you.

It takes great faith and strong will to resist the impact of the civilization that exists on Earth now, on the whole world, and especially on the inhabitants of large cities.

If you are constantly in an environment where discordant music sounds, where the wrong patterns are constantly flashed before your eyes, and where the desires to possess bodies and things are constantly flared up, then your vibrations are constantly on the level where it is impossible for you to hear God. It is impossible to make a distinction between what is right and what is wrong at this level of vibrations.

You are in the swamp of mass consciousness. And if you have only plunged into the swamp for a little while, then there is a chance for you to get out and jump out of the swamp. If you have plunged into the swamp up to your neck, then the hope for your salvation is almost gone.

Each year, millions of victims worshipping the golden calf are added to the garbage heap of history.

Come to think of it, it is the biggest disaster in the history of humankind.

However, we warned you and gave our recommendations 10 years ago when you had just plunged into the swamp.

You have free will. According to the Law of free will, you have made your choice. And the choice was simple and obvious: Either you choose to worship God or you choose to worship the golden calf.

You choose either eternal Life or you choose to stay in the mortal world at the price of your individuality.

As you deprive your soul of the Divine nutrition necessary for it and continue feeding it with the surrogates that the servants of the golden-calf cult are obligingly giving to you 24-hours a day through television, Internet, entertainment, and pleasures, your soul is gradually dying.

The moment comes when you do not have a soul any longer. You become a bio-robot and you have no future.

Everything is determined by your choices, beloved.

If you choose an illusory world according to your free will, it is obvious that you will stay in this world.

If you believe that you only have one life and try to get all pleasures within this life, then you get all the pleasures of this life in exchange for your very Life.

You sell your soul to the devil. Because of all the tinsel and pleasures, you deprive yourselves of an opportunity to continue your Life.

Hardly one person in a thousand living in big cities will be able to prolong his or her evolution as an individualization of God.

All the rest are either dead in the spiritual sense or hopelessly sick, and their souls are at death's door.

This sweet and so funny and careless cult of the golden calf has gathered millions of victims within a short period of time — those who were laid on the altar of service to the golden calf.

Well, at least We have done everything possible from our side in order to show another possible path of development for human civilization.

However, time is unstoppable. And the moment of the final choice has come.

Life or death — everyone chooses by himself.

Nature has to get rid of those individuals who are not capable of further evolution.

The time for reaping has come. The reaping is taking place.

The chaff is being separated from the wheat.

All who are ready to continue the evolution are carefully collected in the Divine reserves.

All who are not ready to continue the evolution will remain in the garbage heap of history.

Therefore, I use this last opportunity so that at least a few people can hear me and return to eternal Life.

Absolutely all of the recommendations were given in Our Messages that We were giving through our Messenger.

Only the dead could not hear that.

I AM Shiva!

About the author

Tatyana Nicholaevna Mickushina was born in the south of western Siberia in the town of Omsk. During all of her life, she has been praying and asking God to grant her an opportunity to work for Him.

In 2004, Tatyana N. Mickushina was granted a Messenger's Mantle of the Great White Brotherhood and received an opportunity to bring the Words of the Masters to people. Since 2005, at certain periods of time, she receives messages from the Ascended Masters in a special way. With the help of many people, the messages have been translated into English and many other languages so that more people can become familiar with them.

"The only thing the Ascended Masters want is to spread their Teaching throughout the world.

The Masters give their messages with the feeling of great Love. Love has no limits.

There are no boundaries between the hearts of people living in different countries; there are no boundaries between the worlds. The boundaries exist only in the consciousness of people.

The Masters appeal through me to every person living on planet Earth.

I wish you success on the spiritual Path!"

Light and Love!
Tatyana Mickushina

Words of **Wisdom**

The first Dictation from Sanat Kumara on March 4, 2005, gave us the following message:

"I AM Sanat Kumara and I have come today to inform the world about a new opportunity and a new dispensation which the Heavens have decided to free through our new Russian Messenger Tatyana.

This turn of events will be unexpected for many of you. Many of you will experience contradictory feelings while reading this message.

However, we do not want to force anybody to believe or not to believe the things to be told. Our task is to give you this knowledge. Its acceptance is a matter of your own free will.

Times have changed and the New Age has come. The worlds have converged. Things which seemed to be an impossible dream a few years ago, even last year, are starting to become real now. We are getting an opportunity to speak through many of you and we are using this opportunity."

Each of the Masters of Wisdom strives to give us what they consider most vital at the present moment of transition. Every message contains the energies of different Masters who give those messages. The Masters speak about the current historical moment on planet Earth. They tell us about energy and vibrations, about the illusion of this world and about the Divine Reality, about the Higher Self of a human and about his lower bodies. They give us concrete recommendations on exactly how to change our own consciousness and continue on the evolutionary Path. It is recommended that you prepare yourself for reading every message very carefully. You have to tune to the Master who is giving the message with the help of proper music, with the help of the Master's image, or by using a prayer or a meditation before reading the message. That way you align your energies, elevate your consciousness, and the messages can benefit you.

SAINT GERMAIN

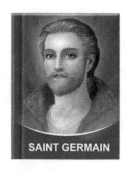

SAINT GERMAIN

Saint Germain is at present an Ascended Master, the Hierarch of the New Age. In his last incarnation as the Count de Saint Germain in the 18th century, he exerted a great influence on the course of world history. The Messages of Master Saint Germain are charged with optimism and faith in the forthcoming

Golden Age! He teaches about preparing for a New Age by transforming our consciousness, and reminds us: "Joy and Love come to you when your Faith is steadfast, when you rely in your consciousness on God and the Ascended Hosts."

SANAT KUMARA

SANAT KUMARA

Masters of Wisdom, first of all Sanat Kumara, remind us about our Divine origin and call us to wake up to a Higher reality, because Divine Reality by its love, wisdom, and beauty exceeds any of the most wonderful aspects of our physical world. The Messages of Sanat Kumara include Teachings on true and false messengers, Communities of the Holy Spirit, responsibility for the duties that one has taken upon him/herself before their incarnation, the right use of the money energy, the choice of everyone between the Eternal and the perishable world, overcoming the ego, the Path of Initiations, and many other topics

MORYA

MORYA

Messages from the Teacher, Master Morya, have been given through Helena Blavatsky in the 19th century, Helena and Nicholas Roerich in the period around 1920-1950, and Mark and Elizabeth Clare Prophet in the 1960's. Master Morya is still actively working on the Spiritual plane to help the humanity of the World. Now the

Masters continue their work through a Messenger from Russia, Tatyana Mickushina.

This book contains selected Messages from Master Morya. Many Teachings are given in the Messages, including the Teachings about the correct actions on the physical plane, Service to Brotherhood, the attainment of the qualities of a disciple such as devotion, persistence, aspiration, and discipline. Some aspects of the Teaching about changing of consciousness are also introduced here.

Author page of T. N. Mickushina on Amazon:

amazon.com/author/tatyana_mickushina

Masters of Wisdom

SHIVA

**Dictations received through the Messenger
Tatyana Nicholaevna Mickushina
from 2005 through 2016**

Tatyana N. Mickushina

Websites:

http://sirius-eng.net (English version)
http://sirius-ru.net (Russian version)

Books by T.N.Mickushina on amazon.com:
amazon.com/author/tatyana_mickushina

CPSIA information can be obtained
at www.ICGtesting.com
Printed in the USA
FSHW021652200319
56529FS